THE ART OF MANAGING BUSINESS EXPECTATIONS

HOW EXPECTATIONS FUNCTION AS THE CURRENCY OF EXECUTION

RODRIGO F. V. MARTIN

Author: Rodrigo F. V. Martin

Title: *The Art of Managing Business Expectations: How Expectations Function as the Currency of Execution*

Paperback ISBN: 979-8-9957321-0-5

Ebook ISBN: 979-8-9957321-1-2

To Adonai, whose authority over my life is the foundation of everything I have built and everything I have learned to release.

For my wife, my daughter, and my son, everything worth building, I built toward you.

For my sweet mother, whose strength I carry.

THE OPERATOR'S CONFESSION

PREFACE

Years ago I sat across from a CEO in Southeast Asia. He had handed me a business bleeding operating margins it could not afford to sustain. Eighteen months later that same business approached two hundred million dollars in revenue. Its valuation multiple had risen six to eight times what it carried when I arrived.

I place that story at the end of this preface. The lesson took time to emerge.

For years before that assignment I operated as a capable executive. I stayed results-oriented, present wherever the work demanded attention, personally closing gaps that would otherwise stall execution. The results confirmed the approach, and that confirmation kept me from asking the question this book explores.

What happens when the organization runs well only because you occupy the room?

I have seen projects stall because two teams interpreted the same commitment differently. Decisions traveled through four layers of management before someone with authority resolved them in minutes. I have entered a conversation, reconnected what had drifted, and seen the organization move forward again. Each time the process felt quick and competent. Each time results continued to arrive.

You have performed these actions hundreds of times. I had done the same.

For many years that pattern defined my professional life. The results confirmed the approach and the approach confirmed itself. The loop closed so cleanly that the structural condition generating the demand for intervention stayed invisible. Dependency conceals itself behind the very outcomes it produces.

I operated inside corporate environments across five countries. When the structure could not carry the expectations placed upon it, capable operators compensated. Informal mechanisms ran alongside the official structure. Work moved through channels that delivered what the system had not yet evolved to sustain. Results arrived consistently. A well-designed system would have prevented the cost.

At the time I had no language for what was happening. I understood performance and pressure. I had not yet seen that execution depends on something more fundamental: expectations must move through the organization, and they must retain their meaning as they travel.

The cost appeared in two places. The first was financial. The second took longer to name.

Leaders and operators absorbed what the system generated but had never been designed to acknowledge. A system designed to carry execution compounds capability. A system sustained through intervention consumes it.

Early in my career, when I led individual teams, the cost of this arrangement remained manageable. As responsibility expanded to business units it multiplied across functions and geographies. By the time I ran entire companies the nature of the role had changed. I no longer operated the ecosystem. I created it.

That shift arrived through the accumulating recognition that what I had done well no longer met the organization's need. Once the shift took hold, the results changed in ways I had not seen before. Operators surfaced execution plans without being asked. The people closest to the work found structural solutions I would never have designed from above. Innovations came through that no amount of centralized involvement could have generated. The system started producing its own intelligence rather than waiting to borrow mine.

What I found when I looked directly at it was this. I had been substituting presence for design. I had tied execution to people rather than to structure. The results were real. They were also evidence of a structural dependency that would outlast any individual's effort to manage it.

This book emerged from that recognition. Execution reliability is a structural property, not primarily a question of effort or capability. It depends on whether expectations have been encoded in a way that allows them to survive distance, time, and organizational load without requiring constant reinforcement. When expectations are encoded correctly, execution continues even when the individuals who once carried it are no longer present in the same way. When they are not, results stay dependent on the continued availability of the people sustaining them.

The chapters that follow are written for leaders whose organizations perform well while remaining dependent on their involvement. Many sense the condition without having named it. The sensing comes before the language, and the language is what this book provides. Once the condition is named it becomes addressable. Until then it persists, because the performance it produces keeps confirming that it should.

The argument moves through several stages. It begins with the conditions that make dependency invisible. It examines the explanations that prevent leaders from recognizing the condition as structural. It introduces the architectural instruments required to resolve it. It describes the governing instruments that regulate execution once the architecture is in place. And it addresses the responsibilities that remain when the system carries the execution the leader once carried alone.

My purpose in writing these pages is simple. I want the reader to recognize the moment that took years for me to understand through experience. Leadership at a certain stage in an organization's growth concerns something other than rescuing outcomes, managing political pressure, or standing in the spotlight that operational heroism generates. The work changes. The transition from operator to architect marks the beginning of a different form of leadership, one in which the leader no longer carries execution personally but builds the environment in which execution flows through the organization itself.

The pages that follow describe how to build it.

HOW TO READ THIS BOOK

I remember the exact moment the pattern first became visible to me. A senior team in The Netherlands had just left a strategy session that felt decisive. Every leader in the room had nodded in agreement. The commitment looked clear on the whiteboard. Yet three weeks later the same decision sat unresolved on my desk. A simple request for clarification had traveled upward through four layers until it reached me. I resolved it in minutes. The work moved again. From the outside the organization still performed. Inside it had learned to wait for my presence before anything decisive could happen.

That single episode repeated itself across countries and business units. Execution rarely stalls in one dramatic failure. It continues to function while it slowly becomes dependent on specific people who step in whenever the structure fails to carry intent from decision into action. The organization keeps delivering results. The dependency deepens beneath the performance. Because the results hold, nothing on the surface signals that a structural condition has begun to take root.

Senior leaders usually encounter this condition through signals that appear ordinary in isolation. A decision that should resolve inside one function moves upward until someone with authority settles it. A stalled initiative regains momentum the moment executive attention focuses on the obstacles around it. A commitment that sounded precise when it was authorized requires repeated clarification as it crosses team boundaries. Each instance registers as leadership engagement. The people involved remain capable and committed. The system keeps producing outcomes. Nothing yet indicates that the structure itself is losing its ability to carry intent reliably across distance and time.

Now, a different pattern emerges. Execution holds together only because certain individuals repeatedly restore the coherence the structure has not preserved. This book begins with that observation. The condition it describes is structural rather than behavioral. Organizations can continue producing acceptable results while they become dependent on intervention to maintain alignment between decisions and outcomes. Because performance continues, the dependency that sustains it often stays unnoticed. Results close the conversation before anyone asks whether the system itself could have carried the work without the intervention that resolved it.

The question that follows is straightforward. What would have to change for execution to remain coherent even when leadership attention shifts elsewhere?

Answering that question requires reading the organization in a different way. Most management discussions explain execution through behavioral categories such as leadership strength, cultural alignment, or employee capability. Those explanations describe how people sustain outcomes even when the underlying structure remains fragile. They do not explain how execution stays reliable once organizational scale extends beyond the reach of individual judgment.

This book approaches the problem from another direction. It treats execution as a structural transmission problem. Intent translates into expectations. Those expectations travel across teams, across time, and across organizational boundaries before they become results. When the meaning of those expectations survives the journey, execution remains coherent. When meaning degrades as it travels, organizations compensate through clarification, escalation, and personal intervention.

Execution reliability depends on whether expectations retain their operational meaning as they move through the organization. That single condition governs more of what organizations experience as execution failure than any behavioral explanation accounts for.

The argument unfolds through a sequence of structural shifts.

In Part I I surface the condition that experienced operators eventually recognize. Organizations can continue performing while individuals carry the coherence the structure does not consistently preserve. The four chapters in this part describe how the dependency forms, why it goes unaddressed, and what it costs once scale amplifies it beyond what personal involvement can sustain.

Part II examines the explanations that allow this condition to persist. Competence, alignment, and strong leadership involvement can sustain results for long periods even when the system itself has not been designed to carry them. These explanations are incomplete. Their incompleteness is what allows the structural condition to go unaddressed while behavioral responses keep producing enough short-term improvement to confirm the diagnosis.

Part III introduces a different way of seeing the organization. Instead of reading the company primarily as a set of functions, the book develops the interface lens. That lens reveals how expectations must survive translation across the boundaries where work moves between teams. Once those boundaries become visible, the question becomes operational rather than diagnostic.

Part IV introduces three governing instruments that regulate execution once work begins moving at scale. Sequence governs the order in which work enters the system. Load governs how much work the system can carry concurrently. Cadence governs how long commitments remain valid as conditions evolve. Together these instruments allow execution reliability to become a property of the system rather than a property of the individuals sustaining it.

Part V examines what leadership becomes once that transition occurs. When the system carries execution, responsibility concentrates at the boundary where structural design ends and judgment begins. The leader does not disappear from this picture. The work the leader does changes in kind.

Some readers will move through the argument sequentially. That is the path the book was designed for. The argument builds on itself. Each part addresses a condition that the previous part has made visible. The governing instruments in Part IV only fully make sense once the diagnostic argument of Parts I and II has been absorbed.

Other readers may begin with Part IV, which describes the governing instruments, and return later to the earlier sections that explain why those instruments become necessary. The book is structured to allow both approaches. The concepts in the later parts are sufficiently self-contained to be read first. The earlier parts deepen them.

What matters most is the question you carry into the first chapter. Most organizations eventually discover that execution depends more on leadership presence than the structure itself can sustain. That discovery usually arrives later than it should. Scale has already converted what was manageable into something structural. The cost of the dependency has been accumulating long enough that addressing it requires more than a change of approach.

The organizations that crossed this boundary first did not have better people. They had leaders who recognized, before scale forced the question, that carrying execution and governing execution are different forms of work. That recognition is the beginning of this book.

CONTENTS

PART ONE
WHEN MANAGEMENT STOPS SCALING

CHAPTER 1
WHEN RESULTS DRIFT BUT NO ONE IS FAILING

THE SYMPTOM

Execution can appear stable while becoming conditional on the continued presence of a few key individuals. The pattern is familiar to any leader who has scaled an organization. Decisions begin to route to the center and coordination requires direct intervention. Commitments that should travel independently start to wait for clarification before anyone acts.

Every organization runs on expectations: they define what should happen, who is responsible, and when someone is authorized to act. When those expectations hold as they travel from decision to delivery, execution is stable. When they lose precision in transit, execution drifts, even when no one is doing anything wrong.

I have lived this pattern across five countries and more than two decades. The meeting ends well, agreement on the project direction, energy in the room, everyone leaving with the same understanding. Two weeks later you are back in a conversation that should not be necessary. The sequence has shifted and the assumptions beneath it have moved. The commitment that seemed clear in the room now needs reconnecting before the work can proceed. You step in, clarify, and the work moves again quickly, competently, without a second thought.

That is exactly the problem.

Most execution failures do not announce themselves through missed targets or visible breakdown. The organization is performing and people are committed. What has shifted is subtler: the amount of involvement required to sustain that output. The pattern repeats in forms every experienced leader recognizes. A decision that should have resolved inside a function arrives at a higher level waiting for someone with broader authority to close it. A handoff between two teams requires a conversation to restore the intent that was supposed to travel with the work. A priority clearly stated in one meeting has to be restated in the next before anyone will move. Each instance looks small and each resolution looks like leadership. Nothing in the surface of results signals what is actually happening. Execution has stopped traveling on its own. It is being carried. The thing carrying it is attention, specifically yours.

I have spent time in rooms where this pattern was already running and nobody in the room had named it yet.

When the structure cannot preserve the meaning of a commitment as it moves across the organization, someone has to do that work manually. Someone reconnects what drifted, clarifies what was assumed, restores the sequence where coordination broke down. The more reliably that person does it, the more reliably the organization learns to wait for it. This is where the dependency becomes invisible, because the intervention works. Results arrive and the organization interprets the pattern as evidence of strong leadership, and it is strong leadership. The problem is that the same behavior keeping execution alive is also the reason the structure never has to get stronger, and every successful rescue postpones the redesign.

The condition is hard to see because the system keeps producing results. Teams remain capable and strategies remain sound; what has changed is the underlying mechanism. Execution has become conditional on presence, on whether the right person is available to hold the system together when it begins to separate.

The increase in leadership involvement feels natural because growth brings complexity, and complexity draws more leadership attention. That explanation has real truth in it. What it conceals is the reason the demand keeps growing. When expectations cannot move through the organization without repeated reinforcement, leadership stops driving execution and starts carrying it. Commitments route through people rather than through structure, usually the same few people who know how to reconnect the system when it fragments. The organization has become dependent, a different condition from weakness, and one with different remedies.

That distinction, dependency versus weakness, was the first thing that had to be named. Every time. Before anything structural could be addressed.

The dependency stayed hidden from the inside longer than anyone would have expected. That consistency, across different industries and different scales, is part of what makes it so difficult to name. People kept patching what the structure could not carry. The patches worked, the structure stayed unaddressed, and that is the pattern's deepest property. The better the people, the longer it hides.

Execution reliability is a question of whether expectations retain their meaning as they travel from decision to delivery, not primarily a question of effort or capability. When meaning survives that journey, execution holds even when leadership attention is elsewhere. When meaning degrades along the way, execution stays fragile regardless of how capable the people sustaining it are.

Organizations can run for a long time without recognizing this. Leaders reconnect expectations, teams absorb ambiguity, and individuals patch what the structure cannot carry. From the outside this looks like resilience. The leader who reconnects execution in a meeting sees the result: work moving again. The team experiences the clarity that follows the gap that made the reconnection necessary goes undetected.

Presence produces results, so presence looks like the answer, and the feedback loop confirms it.

Presence is the symptom of a structural gap, not the answer to it.

As the organization grows, the volume of expectations moving through it increases faster than the informal mechanisms sustaining them. More commitments must travel farther, across more roles and through more layers, before they become results. What worked through proximity breaks down through distance. The involvement that once felt natural becomes the primary constraint on what the organization can reach.

Execution still moves, but it moves because someone is carrying it. The heavier that load gets, the more clearly the structure's absence becomes visible.

Before the condition becomes structural, it announces itself through signals that each look ordinary in isolation. I have seen them appear in the same sequence across organizations in different industries and at different scales, and by the time leaders name them as a pattern, the dependency is already running. The decision that resolved in four minutes at your level had waited three days to reach you. The initiative that regained momentum the week you visited the team softened again the week you did not. The quarterly update from a direct report sounded confident, and you realized afterward you had accepted it without being able to verify what lay beneath it. The handoff between two functions required a clarifying conversation every single time, with no exception, because that conversation was doing the structural work the handoff was supposed to do. The person described as exceptional in a hiring context turned out to mean: exceptional at compensating for what the system cannot carry.

None of these signals announces a crisis. Each one looks like the cost of operating at scale. What I found when I looked at them together, in organization after organization, was that they share a single cause: authority and the work it was supposed to govern had separated, and the separation went unrecorded because someone capable closed the gap before it became a number. The gap was there and the cost was accumulating. The person closing it had simply made it look like leadership rather than like debt.

If you have led through this, you know the specific exhaustion it produces. It is the exhaustion of being the mechanism, of knowing that the system requires your continued presence to stay coherent, a weight of a different kind entirely from the exhaustion of hard work. The work does not stop when you are away. It waits.

I spent years asking the wrong version of that question. The question worth asking is not why leadership keeps intervening. Capable leaders always step in when execution drifts. The question is what it means when the system cannot move without them, and what would have to change for it to carry execution on its own.

CHAPTER 2
THE WRONG DIAGNOSIS

THE CAUSE

When execution starts showing strain, most organizations reach first for explanations they already know how to act on.

I have been in those rooms. The diagnosis arrives quickly and confidently, and it is almost always one of three: the team needs stronger capability, the organization needs renewed motivation, or alignment needs to be reinforced across functions. Each explanation carries a built-in response. Development programs are designed, offsites are scheduled, and communication initiatives are launched. The organization moves again with the reassuring sense that the source of the problem has finally been identified.

Most organizations arrive at the same three conclusions because those conclusions fit the evidence. Capability must be strengthened, because the enterprise has grown more complex. Motivation must be renewed, because energy behind execution has softened. Alignment must be reinforced, because communication across functions has drifted. Each explanation is reasonable, and each produces a response that generates visible activity.

The problem has been postponed, not found.

I have sat in rooms where each of these diagnoses was made with complete confidence, and I have made them myself. They feel right because they correspond to things you can see. The difficulty is that what you can see is being produced by the same system generating the condition. The organization keeps giving you the same signals. You keep responding the same way. The underlying condition learns to survive both.

Several months later the same leaders notice a pattern that feels less like a coincidence and more like a permanent feature of how the organization works. The team appears more capable, energy is higher, and alignment language is sharper. The strain that prompted the intervention is back. Decisions are accumulating at the center again and initiatives slow the moment leadership attention shifts. Conversations that seemed resolved keep reappearing in different forms.

Each of these responses is incomplete rather than wrong, and that distinction is where the real problem lives. Capability, motivation, and alignment describe characteristics of the people inside the system. None of them describe the conditions that govern how work moves through it. When execution strain is read as a people problem, the response strengthens people while leaving the architecture governing their work untouched. The organization ends up with a better-resourced version of the original condition, running the same structural gap with more people absorbing what the structure cannot carry.

A capability review makes this most concrete. Performance gaps are identified, development plans are created, and training investments are expanded. Managers become more skilled and more confident. Then the same conversation returns several months later, sometimes with different people in the same seats, and the organization concludes that capability still needs strengthening. The reasoning feels proportionate. When decisions arrive late or come out inconsistent, the assumption that complexity has exceeded competence fits what you are seeing. What it overlooks is the relationship between competence and structural ambiguity.

When ambiguity originates in the coordination architecture rather than in the ability of individuals, increasing competence produces people more capable of absorbing it rather than eliminating it. Managers become the informal transfer mechanism for work the system was never designed to carry reliably. They reconcile conflicting expectations, clarify incomplete commitments, and repair handoffs that formal processes failed to carry. Execution continues because capable people compensate for what the structure was never designed to hold.

I ran a capability program across a commercial leadership team early in that role. The team improved. The structural condition was untouched. What the program had produced was a more capable set of people absorbing the same structural ambiguity. The ambiguity itself was untouched. The system had become better at hiding its own weakness.

The organization had become better at absorbing ambiguity without becoming better at eliminating it. That distinction matters because an organization good at absorbing ambiguity has no incentive to redesign the system generating it; people keep the work moving, and that is precisely what keeps the condition hidden.

The people filling the gaps make the gaps invisible.

The motivation explanation runs the same cycle everywhere I have seen it deployed. An offsite generates genuine enthusiasm, priorities are reaffirmed, and conversations intensify. For several weeks the organization looks revitalized. Then execution returns to its previous pattern, and the response is to sustain the energy through reinforcement: renewed purpose, more communication, sharper accountability conversations. Motivation determines what people bring to their work. Whether that work moves coherently through the organization once it leaves their hands depends on something different. Energy originates within individuals, but transfer depends on the architecture connecting them. When the structure carrying commitments across functions is weak, increased motivation accelerates the movement of ambiguity rather than resolving it. The only thing that has changed is the pace at which it circulates.

The alignment explanation outlasted both of the others precisely because it comes closest to describing something structural and that is what makes it the most damaging. It creates the strongest illusion that the real problem has been addressed. Strategic meetings conclude with genuine consensus, language is clarified, and priorities are agreed. Leaders leave the room confident that direction has been established. Then execution begins, and the meaning of those commitments has to travel across boundaries that do not share the same context. Each function interprets the same direction through the constraints of its own responsibilities. The divergence develops gradually, often undetected until results expose the divergence that no one detected in the meeting. The organizations that ran this cycle longest were the last to examine the alignment explanation and the last to revise it.

A commercial operation spanning multiple countries and time zones made this concrete. The strategic direction had been agreed and the language was clear. Six weeks into execution, three functions were running three different interpretations of the same priority, each defensible within their own domain and each in conflict with the others at the point where the work had to converge. The meeting had produced agreement and nothing more. The alignment had existed in the room and nowhere else.

Alignment at scale is a verification problem, not a conversational one. Conversation can establish agreement at the moment commitments are expressed. Conversation cannot ensure that the meaning of those commitments survives the journey through functions, time horizons, and operational constraints. When leaders cannot verify whether intent has been translated into consistent operational meaning across those boundaries, agreement becomes the only available signal of coordination. Under those conditions, organizations substitute affirmation for evidence. Confident updates, fluent recaps, and well-formed commitments begin standing in for shared interpretation, even though interpretation is precisely what expands as complexity increases.

Senior leaders govern work they cannot observe directly. The individuals closest to execution hold the most accurate understanding of operational constraints, yet those constraints are difficult to surface openly because doing so may trigger intervention, loss of autonomy, or forced trade-offs that cannot be resolved in the meeting. Both sides adapt without deliberate intent. Managers learn to present confident narratives that preserve autonomy. Leaders learn to evaluate those narratives because they have no independent means of inspecting the operational conditions beneath them. The signals are the same wherever this dynamic runs: the direct report who leads with confidence while burying the constraint inside a subordinate clause, the functional head who has learned that 'we are on track with some risks we are managing' preserves autonomy while 'we have a structural conflict that requires a decision' triggers immediate escalation. The phrase "on track" drifts from a claim tied to verifiable criteria into a reassurance that maintains coherence in the room.

Alignment becomes something the organization performs rather than something it can verify.

The theater does not emerge from deception or cynicism. It emerges because the organization lacks a basis for determining whether commitments carry the same operational meaning across its boundaries. People speak in confident commitments because leadership asks for confidence, because ambiguity carries professional risk, and because the system receiving the commitment cannot independently verify what lies beneath it. The behavior is entirely rational. The problem in this case is structural and behavior rational. The people are responding exactly as the system teaches them to.

These explanations persist because they are incomplete: close enough to the evidence to feel accurate, far enough from the cause to leave the structural condition unchanged. Development programs do strengthen individuals and motivation initiatives do increase visible energy. Alignment sessions do produce consensus that temporarily resolves confusion. Each generates activity that reads as progress, and the feedback loop is powerful: effort produces movement, movement produces outcomes, and outcomes confirm the diagnosis that generated the effort. The condition learns to survive the response.

Agreement is not alignment.

Agreement is the moment a commitment is expressed. Alignment exists only when the system can verify that intent has been translated into consistent operational meaning across roles, time horizons, and competing incentives. When leaders cannot inspect that translation independently of the people reporting it, conversation cannot govern execution regardless of how frequent or disciplined it becomes. The organization lacks a system through which intent can travel with preserved meaning, accountability can hold without reinforcement, and execution can be verified independently of the individuals who currently sustain it.

That absence is structural.

The three diagnoses share one common property: they locate the problem inside people. They assume that if capability is raised, motivation is renewed, or alignment is reinforced, execution will improve. The structural question is different. It asks what the system was never designed to carry. When expectations cannot survive the distance between the room where they are formed and the execution layer where they must be delivered without losing precision, people will always be required to reconstruct them. That is a transmission problem, not a people problem at all.

What becomes possible when the frame shifts is a reorientation in what the organization looks at. The organization that reads its execution failures as transmission problems no longer asks who failed but where meaning changed. It no longer asks what people lack but what the design was never built to hold. That shift in what the organization looks at is where the structural answer begins.

The next two chapters name the specific mechanisms.

CHAPTER 3
THE FOUR MINUTE RESOLUTION

THE CONSEQUENCE

A difficult issue can sit unresolved for days even when every piece of information needed to solve it already exists inside the organization. Escalation eventually delivers the answer, but the delay itself reveals something deeper: authority is not reaching the work at the pace the work requires.

I lived this reality one evening in Kyiv. More than one hundred containers sat outside a processing plant in Brazil, ready to move, while the commercial clock ran. The cargo had already been sold, documentation was in order, and logistics had coordinated the transportation schedule. Clients were expecting the shipments to depart on time. An interpretation question inside the inspection process had halted the release. The people responsible for the plant understood the urgency and had been working to resolve it for days. The logistics team had contacted regulatory specialists. Managers had attempted to clarify the requirement through several channels. The interpretation that would allow the inspection to proceed had simply not reached the inspectors responsible for releasing the shipments.

That evening I was having dinner in Kyiv at the Brazilian ambassador's residence with the Secretary of Agriculture when my COO called. He explained the situation: one hundred containers stuck at the plant, five days of discussions, no resolution. I raised the issue across the table, clarified the interpretation behind the requirement, and the Secretary placed a call to the head inspector in Brazil. Minutes later the inspectors received the confirmation they needed. The cargo began moving.

From the perspective of the organization, the episode was straightforward. A difficult issue had been escalated, someone with the appropriate authority had resolved it quickly, and the operational problem was closed. That reading of the event is accurate, and it misses the more important thing.

The plant understood the documentation, the logistics team understood the shipments, and the commercial team understood what was at stake. Every piece of information required to release the cargo already existed inside the organization. What the inspectors lacked was authority: the authorization to confirm the interpretation behind the requirement and act on it.

Five days of discussions measured a failure of transmission. The authority required to finalize a straightforward interpretation had no structural path to the people who needed it, and so it waited until someone at a dinner in Kyiv happened to be sitting next to the right person.

That is luck with a competent person attached to it. It also felt like exactly the right thing to do. That feeling is the problem.

Situations like this appear in different forms across every growing organization. A contract negotiation stalls, a delivery schedule stays uncertain, or a client commitment sits unresolved, and in each case escalation closes the issue quickly. The leader reconnects the expectation, the decision becomes clear, and the organization resumes its movement. In each case, the speed of that resolution conceals the same underlying fact.

What looks like leadership speed at the top often measures something different: the distance between where authority lives and where work needed it. A decision that takes four minutes at the top usually waited days for authority to reach it. That gap is what the four-minute resolution names.

The change was always gradual enough that no one scheduled it, and visible enough in retrospect that no one could explain why it had gone unnamed. Questions that should have resolved close to the work begin appearing at higher levels with increasing regularity. Coordination calls require the presence of executives whose authority allows them to reconnect fragmented expectations. Operational momentum stabilizes when those individuals are available and softens when their attention shifts elsewhere. The escalation path becomes the operating path. The organization keeps performing, and the continuity of that performance becomes tied to the availability of the specific individuals capable of reconnecting the system when it separates.

The moment of recognition is the same every time. The issue that required two levels of escalation last quarter now requires three. The coordination call that once needed a director now needs a VP. Nobody scheduled this change and nobody decided that authority should concentrate upward. The system learned it because escalation kept working, and what works becomes the path.

I saw the same mechanism expressed differently while working with several international offices across Europe. The strategic direction had been agreed and information had been cascaded clearly to each business unit, which had structured its operational plan accordingly. Under normal conditions, planning templates arrived in mid-October. Teams completed their plans by mid-November and returned them to headquarters for approval. Final confirmation arrived in early December, allowing execution to begin as the new cycle opened.

That year, authorization arrived several weeks late. By then the operating window built into the original plans had already begun to close. The strategy was unchanged and market conditions were largely the same.

Authority had simply reached the teams too late for full deployment. Hiring accelerated beyond plan to make up lost time. Retail and foodservice chains had already filled category slots. Logistics contracts were negotiated under pressure, at higher prices. What had been designed as a deliberate market entry became a sequence of accelerated adjustments, each one correcting for the time lost waiting for authorization to arrive. Distribution was ultimately secured because the portfolio offered a stronger value proposition than competitors had placed in the market.

What I found in that market, and in every similar situation I traced afterward, was that the gap between when authority should have arrived and when it did arrive was measurable in lost commercial weeks, not in organizational failures that anyone would have recognized as structural. The outcome looked like operational complexity and market variability. The primary cause was authority arriving after the window it needed to reach.

If the diagnosis is market variability, the response is better forecasting. If the diagnosis is operational complexity, the response is more coordination. If the diagnosis is authority latency, the response is a different question entirely: what would have to change for decisions to move through the organization at the same speed the market demands? Most organizations reach the first two diagnoses because they fit the evidence and point toward responses the organization already knows how to execute. The actual cause stays unnamed and therefore unaddressed.

When the escalation path became permanent, the crossing point arrived earlier than anyone expected. The organization that appeared to be scaling had in fact been learning to route more and more of its decisions through the same narrow channel. That channel worked. It kept working. The fact that it was consuming something irreplaceable did not appear in any number the organization was measuring.

At small scale, the escalation arrangement holds and leaders remain close to the work. Shared context allows informal conversation to restore alignment quickly. The speed of intervention more than compensates for the structural gap it reveals. The organization grows, and the leader's involvement looks like the reason.

At a certain scale, that relationship inverts. The same personal carrying that once accelerated the organization begins consuming the capacity that would otherwise drive it. Escalation volume that leadership was absorbing as a natural part of the role now occupies the attention that strategic sensing, directional judgment, and system design require. The organization keeps performing while losing its capacity to expand, because the mechanism carrying execution has become the ceiling on what execution can reach. The inflection point between those two conditions is the moment leadership shifts from accelerant to constraint. Most organizations cross it without recognizing it, because the performance that conceals the dependency also conceals the crossing.

You know this moment. The coordination call you should not have needed to attend. The decision that waited three days for thirty minutes of your attention. The quarter that required more of your involvement than the one before it, despite nothing obvious having changed. Each instance looks like a one-time problem. In sequence they are evidence that authority is not reaching the work at the pace the work requires.

Once that pattern becomes visible, the question it raises has a specific shape. The question is not how to intervene faster but what would allow authority to reach the work without requiring the intervention at all.

CHAPTER 4
SHADOW SYSTEMS: HOW TEAMS SURVIVE STRUCTURAL ABSENCE

THE CYCLE

Across five countries and more than two decades, they were present before I arrived and running more load than anyone had measured. A spreadsheet that only one person fully understands becomes the real source of truth when the official report proves unreliable. A quiet conversation before the formal meeting makes the meeting itself productive. An email thread between two functions resolves the question the agenda never managed to settle. None of these mechanisms appear in the organization's formal design. Without them, the work would stall.

Informal networks appear inside every organization. They sustain execution when the formal system cannot carry the expectations placed upon it. These networks exist because the official design falls short, and because they work, no one is in a hurry to replace them.

When formal structures cannot reliably carry the expectations placed upon them, organizations develop shadow systems. These are informal networks of relationships, workarounds, and private coordination habits that keep execution moving outside the official architecture. Shadow systems rarely emerge through deliberate design. They appear as individuals respond to practical constraints inside their roles. When an approval process slows decisions that must move quickly, someone learns which conversation resolves the issue faster. When a handoff between two functions repeatedly produces confusion, someone builds a private checklist to ensure the next step begins correctly. When commitments arrive incomplete, experienced operators learn to translate the intent behind them before passing the work forward, each adjustment locally rational. These adjustments accumulate into a parallel operating structure that the organization neither documents nor governs.

The effect this creates is subtle, and that subtlety is precisely the problem. When shadow systems compensate successfully for structural gaps, results continue to arrive without revealing how they were produced. Performance measures hold steady and the formal process appears reliable. The informal network has absorbed the variance that would otherwise expose the weakness in the design. The organization receives the outcome without receiving the signal that redesign is required.

In my experience, the approval patterns I encountered most often were not the ones documented in the process. They were the informal paths that experienced operators had built around the documented ones. Procurement processes make this concrete. The documented procedure requires purchase requests to pass through several approval layers before orders are finalized. Experienced managers know which approvals rarely affect the decision. They confirm the relevant information through informal conversation before the request ever enters the system. When the formal process begins it proceeds smoothly because the essential coordination already occurred elsewhere. From the perspective of leadership, the process looks efficient. What leadership cannot see is the informal coordination that made it possible, because it happened outside the system leadership can observe.

In my experience, the people who build these workarounds are almost always the most capable and most committed people in the organization. They built them because they cared about outcomes and the formal system was failing to deliver. That combination of competence and care makes shadow systems nearly undetectable from above, because the results they produce look indistinguishable from results the system produced on its own.

As shadow systems develop, they accumulate expertise that exists nowhere in formal documentation. The individuals operating inside these networks develop shared language, intuitive coordination habits, and practical understanding of how to navigate the gaps between formal expectations and operational reality. They become effective precisely because they have learned how the organization actually works, not how its diagrams say it should. This expertise grows more important as organizations scale. Expansion introduces more functions, more locations, and more layers of management. Each boundary expectations must cross is another opportunity for delay, reinterpretation, or loss of meaning. the outcome, most of the times was that the people holding it became the only reliable path between functions, as the structure had left no other route.

The consequences become visible most clearly when the informal carriers of execution change. A key operator leaves and the team discovers that what appeared to be a documented process was maintained in practice by that individual's knowledge and relationships. A period of rapid growth overwhelms the informal network because the people coordinating the work cannot absorb additional complexity. A senior leader who frequently reconnects commitments across functions becomes unavailable and coordination begins to falter. Each situation reveals the same underlying condition. The continuity of execution depended on people whose knowledge existed outside the formal structure of the enterprise. When those people are no longer available, the structure has no way to replace what they carried.

This exposure played out across operations in Europe, Asia, and Brazil. The pattern is always the same: everything looked fine until it did not. When it stopped looking fine, the problem turned out to have been there for years, invisible because someone capable had been absorbing it.

The distinction between shadow systems and healthy informal coordination lives in what drives the behavior. Healthy organizations encourage initiative beyond formal boundaries. People collaborate across functions, adapt when conditions change, and find better paths than the ones originally designed. That describes a functioning organization learning and improving. Shadow systems appear when individuals must compensate for structural absence in order to protect outcomes. Collaboration fills gaps the organization has left open intentionally or is actively working to close. Shadow systems fill gaps the organization has never mapped, and filling them prevents the signal that would expose them.

Each time this arrangement stabilize, the signal that should have forced redesign was the first thing it consumed. Shadow systems suppress the signal that would expose the structural absence they are compensating for. That suppression is their deeper cost. They conceal the condition they appear to be solving.

Variance is the most valuable diagnostic information inside a complex enterprise. It reveals where expectations lose clarity as they move across organizational boundaries. When shadow systems absorb that variance before it becomes visible, the organization loses the information required to strengthen its architecture. Interfaces that require redesign stay unchanged because someone has learned to bridge them. Commitments that arrive incomplete keep circulating because someone habitually clarifies them. Decisions that should resolve locally keep escalating because someone with authority is available to close them quickly.

Organizations adapt to this arrangement with surprising fluency. Teams rely on relationships rather than formal handoffs. Managers rely on personal judgment rather than distributed authority. Capable individuals compensate for design conditions the structure has not yet evolved to carry, and the arrangement appears stable precisely because it continues to work. The enterprise loses the feedback required to strengthen its own architecture. The organization grows while the design responsible for carrying execution stays unchanged, because the people filling the gaps have made the gaps invisible.

Variance that should expose a design limitation gets converted into performance by the individuals capable of absorbing it. The organization receives the outcome without receiving the information that would explain how the outcome was produced. Performance confirms the belief that the system is functioning, which directs corrective attention toward the people sustaining execution rather than toward the architecture governing it. Those same people strengthen their capacity to compensate, allowing performance to continue while the structural absence stays unchanged.

The cost I found accumulating under these conditions had a specific character that did not show up in any performance report. The loop is self-reinforcing. Its cost accumulates in ways that performance dashboards do not capture. Leadership attention starts flowing to decisions that should travel independently. Operational fatigue exceeds what the actual workload would justify. Trust in judgment begins to erode because alignment has to be recreated repeatedly rather than carried forward by the architecture.

Shadow systems can be found before a departure forces the discovery. I have used the same three signals across organizations in different industries and at different scales, and in every case they surfaced the informal load the formal structure was not carrying. The first: look for the two or three people who appear in every cross-functional coordination thread regardless of the functional topic. Their presence is the interface, not a sign of engagement; they are standing at a boundary the design never governed. The second: identify the process steps that complete faster when certain people are in the room and slower when they are not. When the pace of a formal process depends on whether a specific individual is present to guide it through, the process was never actually built. The third: find the documentation that exists but has never been run without the person who wrote it standing beside it. The pattern held every time I traced it: the document described what the formal process should do and the person showed what it actually took to make that happen. The gap between the two was the shadow system.

A shadow system identified before departure is a structural gap that can be designed. A shadow system identified after departure is a structural gap that must be rebuilt. The difference between those two moments is the discipline of reading what is working and asking why.

If you have led through a key departure or a reorganization, you know this moment. What everyone believed was a process turned out to be a person. Someone who knew how to make things move, running an informal system nobody had thought to document because nobody had needed to. The process had never actually been built.

That moment of exposure is also an opportunity, if the organization is willing to read it correctly. Every shadow system is a precise diagnosis. This is what the formal system cannot carry, and here is the workaround built to carry it instead. Reading those workarounds as information rather than as solutions is where structural design begins.

The people running those workarounds are not the problem to be solved. They are the most reliable signal of where the design has failed. When the formal architecture finally arrives, the operators who built the shadow systems will be the first to know whether it actually works, because they still remember what it replaced. Their adoption is not a training problem. It is a design test.

PART TWO

THE EXPLANATIONS THAT FAIL AT SCALE

CHAPTER 5
THE COMPETENCE TRAP: WHEN CAPABILITY REPLACES ARCHITECTURE

THE COMPETENCE

Early in my time running a business unit, an experienced director change the trajectory of an entire production operation in a matter of weeks. The organization celebrated it as strong leadership. The celebration was correct, but what it missed was more important.

Production planning across the facilities had been set conservatively for years, because the system gave plant managers no reliable read on what the commercial organization could actually absorb. Facilities ran below potential. Contracts accumulated on the commercial side while production sat underutilized. Then the market shifted. Relationships matured, volumes contracted, and commitments began outrunning the production assumptions that had originally defined capacity. The constraint moved from the commercial side to the production side, and the system had not been built to detect that change, let alone respond to it.

For two weeks before the director stepped in, the plants operated in quiet paralysis while commercial commitments kept arriving. Plant managers knew the volume had increased, yet they had no cross-functional picture that would allow them to adjust schedules or staffing without central approval. Each day the backlog grew by a measurable amount. The cost showed up as delayed shipments, contracts placed at risk, and key customer relationships absorbing silent pressure. The teams were competent, the equipment was reliable and fully utilized, and the processes were documented and followed. The system had no mechanism to translate commercial reality into operational reality without waiting for one person to bridge the gap.

That is a talented individual filling the space where a management system should be.

Most organizations respond to this pattern by reaching a conclusion that feels proportionate: if decisions require repeated clarification, strengthen the competence of the people providing that clarification. The logic follows from what is visible. Ambiguity exists. Experienced individuals resolve it, and the organization reads the outcome as progress. What the logic leaves unexamined is whether the ambiguity should exist at all. Competence is being applied not to extend the organization's reach but to reconstruct conditions the system was expected to preserve on its own. The organization is compensating for a structural problem with its best people, continuously, and calling that management.

The stronger the people, the longer the structure can avoid being built.

In a business unit of meaningful scale, the structural gap sustained by competent individuals typically consumes fifteen to twenty-five percent of senior leadership time in reconstructing clarity that architecture should have preserved. That time appears in no budget and shows up in no performance review. I tracked where my own week actually went across one quarter leading a large commercial operation. More than a third of it was reconstruction work that a designed system would have made unnecessary. The breakdown was specific: decisions delegated two weeks earlier returning for confirmation because the context required to finalize them had never been transferred; cross-functional commitments requiring a clarifying conversation before any action could begin; priorities restated in one meeting that had to be restated again in the next. None of it registered as structural cost. It registered as normal leadership activity, and that normalization is precisely what kept it from registering as a cost. The cost accumulated in the quiet displacement of the work that only leadership altitude can perform: external sensing, directional judgment, and the design decisions that determine what the next year looks like.

The signals arrive before anyone names the pattern. The calendars of the most experienced people fill first because clarity routes to where context exists. Work that has been delegated returns for confirmation because the context required to finalize it was never transferred with the decision itself. Commitments that appeared precise when expressed arrive at execution with enough interpretive drift that someone has to re-anchor them before work can continue. The organization keeps moving, and each movement requires intervention to sustain it.

I ran a capability program across a commercial leadership team early in that same role. The team was genuinely stronger six months later: better decisions, faster responses, more confidence at the boundaries between functions. Then the same coordination problems returned, handled now with more skill but still requiring the same personal involvement to resolve. The same conversation came back. Different faces in some of the seats, same structural positions. The people had improved. The system had not. What the program produced was a more capable set of people absorbing the same structural ambiguity. The ambiguity itself was untouched. The same pattern, seen from a different layer, had a different look but the same cause.

An organization that becomes better at absorbing ambiguity has no incentive to redesign the system generating it. This same pattern run for years inside organizations that, by every external measure, appeared to be functioning well. The variance never showed in any report. It showed when someone capable left and the organization discovered, in the weeks that followed, that what it had believed was a process had in fact been a person.

As the organization scales, this arrangement becomes harder to see and more expensive to carry. Expectations must travel across more roles, functions, and time horizons before they become results. Decisions no longer depend solely on being correct at the moment they are made. They depend on whether the meaning behind those decisions remains consistent as they move through the organization. When that meaning is preserved only through individual judgment rather than structural design, those individuals become the restoration mechanism. They spend their capacity rebuilding what the system cannot hold rather than multiplying what it can.

Work has to pass through expertise rather than through structure before it can advance. Judgment consumed at the point of use leaves no residue in the system. Each problem solved leaves the organization exactly as dependent as before, because the organization knows problems have been solved but cannot reproduce those solutions independently. They lived in people rather than in design.

The behavioral signals of this condition are rational at the individual level and corrosive at the organizational level. Managers defer interpretation upward not from incapacity but from the reasonable calculation that acting on ambiguous authority introduces more risk than waiting for validated meaning. Initiative narrows because deviation requires justification. Teams grow cautious because waiting for authorized interpretation is reliably safer than exercising judgment independently. By the point of first recognition, those patterns were already well established. That is what makes them so costly to address, they arrive before anyone has language for them. What I found, each time, was that the people exhibiting them were not disengaged. They were responding exactly as the system had taught them to.

The competence trap persists precisely because success reinforces it. Each resolved ambiguity confirms the routing pattern through which judgment currently travels. Each avoided failure delays the need to examine whether the system itself should carry the knowledge that individuals are supplying. The organization loses the ability to distinguish between the quality of its people and the adequacy of its design, because both produce the same visible result: work moves, outcomes arrive, performance holds.

The question that breaks the trap is simple to state and difficult to face. Would those outcomes still arrive if the individuals currently sustaining them were unavailable? When the answer is uncertain, competence has already become dependency rather than an asset.

The rescues are not dramatic. They are quiet and competent, and they are completely invisible in any performance report the organization produces. A senior leader steps into the room and the alignment that should have existed already suddenly appears. Everyone leaves satisfied. Nobody asks how many times that same clarification has been required.

A leader who performs well under pressure is valuable. A system that requires performance under pressure as a routine condition of execution requires redesign. One describes a person. The other describes a structural condition. Until an organization can hold that distinction clearly, it will keep consuming its best people to sustain a design it has never stopped to examine.

Test this in your own organization on Monday. Identify the last three cross-functional decisions that required escalation to your level or the level above you. For each one, ask a single question: would that decision have resolved at the point of work if the system had carried the expectation without loss of meaning? If the answer is no for more than one of the three, the competence trap is operating. The structure is still being carried by people rather than carrying the work itself. The cost of that arrangement does not appear in any number you are currently watching. It appears when one of those people leaves.

CHAPTER 6
GHOST RESPONSIBILITY

THE AUTHORSHIP

Most organizations, when they discover execution is being carried by capable individuals rather than the system, reach for the same remedy. They decide to strengthen the capability of those individuals. Chapter 5 showed why that remedy falls short. People filling structural gaps become more capable at filling them, and the gap itself stays invisible.

Capability is only part of what those individuals are carrying. The other part is authorship. Operators across most organizations are delivering results derived from plans they had no part in constructing. Targets arrive from above with expectations communicated clearly enough to establish pressure. Performance is measured against numbers that appear reasonable from the leadership level. The step that converts those expectations into something an operator can actually own has been omitted so consistently that most organizations no longer notice its absence.

This condition has a name. Ghost responsibility.

Ghost responsibility appears whenever operators are held accountable for outcomes that originate entirely outside the layer responsible for executing them. The logic connecting daily decisions to the final objective has been constructed at the leadership level and assigned to an operational level that had no hand in building it. The tell is consistent: the people carrying the accountability could describe their targets precisely and their authority only vaguely. The organization believes it has distributed responsibility across those who deliver it. What it has actually distributed is expectation: pressure to perform against plans that were never theirs to shape.

Accountability travels through the organization. Ownership does not follow.

I encountered this condition directly in Moscow while responsible for developing export markets for a large international company. The organization had significant scale, experienced leadership, and an ambitious plan to expand into the Russian and CIS markets. At the leadership level the strategic objective had already been defined. Production volumes were known. Plants in Brazil were preparing shipments. The commercial office in Moscow received a straightforward mandate: sell the product that would arrive every month.

Approximately thirty thousand tons of protein product would enter the market each month. Prices were communicated. Spreadsheets circulated showing expected volumes. The commercial team understood its role clearly: ensure the market absorbs the production arriving from Brazil. From the perspective of leadership the expectation appeared simple. Capable operators, strong demand, and clear targets already in place. If the commercial organization performed, the volumes would move.

The missing element was invisible from that vantage point.

The sales organization was structured around distinct commercial channels: wholesale distributors, retail chains, and trading partners capable of absorbing large quantities when necessary. The people running those channels understood their markets and maintained relationships capable of sustaining stable demand. What the thirty thousand tons required, a structured allocation of volume across those channels before execution began, had never been constructed with their participation.

Rather than starting with a structured allocation of volume across those channels, execution started with production. The plant would indicate what was being shipped and when it would depart Brazil. Only after that information arrived would the commercial organization begin searching for customers capable of absorbing the available product, running the entire system in reverse. The commercial organization was chasing production rather than operating its channels. Customers were approached based on what the plant happened to have available rather than based on a deliberate allocation built around the structure of demand in the market.

Responsibility existed without authorship.

The effect took months to become fully visible. The market kept absorbing product and the commercial office remained active. What became apparent was the instability underneath. Monthly execution ranged from relatively smooth to heavily improvised with no structural variable to explain the difference.

Production numbers arrived before commercial allocation existed. Operators shifted into reaction mode immediately, calling customers without a structured sequence, prioritizing whoever could absorb volume fastest rather than whoever fit the long-term channel strategy. Discount conversations appeared earlier in the cycle than they should have because inventory risk translated directly into pricing pressure. Logistics began compressing timelines to match commercial uncertainty, and documentation errors increased because shipments were being assigned after negotiation rather than before it. By week four came operational recovery, and then the cycle started again. Volumes moved and revenue was recorded month after month while the underlying instability compounded beneath both.

The people inside the system were committed and skilled. The structural absence was not visible from their positions because they were inside it, absorbing it, keeping it functional through effort alone.

I built the structure inside my own responsibilities because the formal system was not going to produce it on its own. I started mapping expected production against the commercial channels in the Russian market, identifying which customers could reliably absorb particular product cuts, which segments required stable supply, and how volumes could be distributed across wholesale, retail, food service, and trading partners before shipments left Brazil, without any formal mandate to do so. It was a discipline I introduced inside my own scope so that execution would stop depending entirely on improvisation.

The difference became visible within a quarter. Sales grew more predictable. Negotiations with customers became easier because we were approaching them with a structured offer rather than a volume problem. The rhythm of execution stabilized because the market was no longer reacting exclusively to production.

Some colleagues recognized the logic and tried similar practices. Without a formal system supporting the approach the results stayed uneven. The commercial plan existed only at the leadership level, so the information required to sustain the structure never reached the people who needed it to operate. The discipline remained personal rather than systemic, and personal disciplines are fragile for a reason that became clear only later. They leave when the person does.

What that experience revealed is a condition far more common than most organizations recognize. Strategy stops at the leadership layer while responsibility continues downward into operations. The opportunity to construct the logic connecting targets to stable execution stays above while the pressure to deliver against those targets travels down. The organization believes it has distributed responsibility. What it has actually distributed is expectation.

Ghost responsibility is the condition in which operators carry the weight of results derived from plans they had no hand in constructing. Activity stays high. Commitment stays strong. Execution grows reactive because the structural path connecting strategy to operations has never been built by the people responsible for walking it. Operators were doing exactly what the design required. The design is what needed to change

The fix is architectural. Until operators participate in building the plan, responsibility circulates as an expectation imposed from above rather than a structure owned by the layer responsible for delivering it. When authorship enters the system, the character of execution changes in the same direction, every time. Operators stop reacting and start anticipating. Commitments stabilize because the structure finally gives people something real to stand on rather than a target to absorb.

The behavior producing ghost responsibility is entirely rational at the individual level. Leaders communicate targets because the business requires execution. Operators absorb pressure because the work must continue moving. The problem is the system that makes this behavior rational. The people are responding exactly as the design requires them to. What the organization lacks is a mechanism through which responsibility can settle into authorship rather than circulating as accountability without structural grounding. The design is what needs to change, and that change is the subject of Part III.

PART THREE
SEEING THE ORGANIZATION AS A SYSTEM

CHAPTER 7
MANAGEMENT ARCHITECTURE: SEEING THE BUSINESS AS A SYSTEM

THE PERCEPTION

The organizational chart shows who reports to whom and what each function owns. It describes the structure accurately at that level. Execution does not live in those boxes. Execution happens in the movement of expectations across the boundaries where those boxes meet.

This is the governing distinction of Part III. It changes what the organization has to build if it wants execution to become reliable rather than dependent on the individuals currently sustaining it. The preceding chapters named the conditions that produce dependency: the competence trap, ghost responsibility, and the heroism tax. Each of those conditions is visible from the outside. What produced them is not, because what produced them lives in the connections between functions, not inside the functions themselves.

A commitment becomes a result only after it has traveled through multiple domains whose knowledge, incentives, and constraints differ from those present when the commitment was first made. Commercial intent must translate into operational sequence, product design into deliverable capability, and financial assumptions into economic outcomes that survive real conditions. Each translation requires meaning to survive movement across a boundary where the context that gave that meaning its precision is no longer fully present. When that meaning survives, execution is coherent. When meaning degrades, the organization compensates through intervention, escalation, and the judgment of people standing at the boundaries where meaning is being lost.

That compensation is exactly what Parts I and II described. The pattern looks like a people problem from inside the functions. It is a boundary problem in the connections between them.

This distinction became visible in a specific way that I did not expect the first time I encountered it clearly, and in every organization since it has taken the same form. A commercial team and an operations team in a consumer goods business were coordinating weekly. Both were competent and both were active. The commercial director called his operations counterpart every Thursday, not because the formal process required it, but because that call was the only mechanism through which their shared assumptions about timing, volume, and delivery were kept aligned. The call was not the interface; it was the substitute for an interface that had never been designed. When the commercial director traveled for two weeks without finding a replacement rhythm, the assumptions kept moving on each side without the other knowing. By the time I traced the resulting delivery variance backward, the divergence had been accumulating for eleven days before anyone detected it. Both functions had been performing correctly within their own domain throughout. The boundary between them had no design, only a habit, and when the habit broke, the boundary failed. What I found when I looked directly at it was an architectural absence, not a coordination problem.

The functional lens through which most organizations read themselves obscures this distinction almost completely. Performance is evaluated inside functions because measurement is possible there, with sales through pipeline conversion and revenue growth, operations through throughput and delivery reliability, and finance through margin discipline and capital allocation. When each domain appears competent and active, the organization concludes that its operating capacity is sound.

That conclusion holds only when the distance between functions is small enough for shared context and informal coordination to preserve the meaning of commitments as they move. The failure mode at scale is multiplicative rather than additive. Coherence becomes a property of the connections between functions rather than of the functions themselves. An organization can have strong sales, strong operations, strong finance, and strong product development while still producing outcomes that are inconsistent, delayed, or expensive to recover. The failure originates at the translation points between functions, not within the functions themselves.

Execution behaves multiplicatively at boundaries.

A five percent interpretation error at the commercial-to-operations boundary combined with a five percent error at the operations-to-logistics boundary does not produce a five percent outcome problem. It produces something larger and less predictable because each error creates the conditions for the next one. The stacking happens before anyone can see it. By the time variance surfaces as a result, two or three boundary errors have already accumulated.

This becomes concrete when outcomes that no single function caused also prove resistant to correction within any single function. A commercial commitment made against a delivery timeline that operations never validated. A pricing structure approved without visibility into the margin implications that finance will discover weeks later. A product decision that introduces dependencies only visible when multiple teams attempt to deliver simultaneously. Each function acted competently according to the information available within its own domain. The combined outcome reveals misalignment that no function individually created and no function alone can resolve.

What failed was the medium through which intent traveled between them.

The distortion extends into how responsibility is interpreted, which is where the economic cost becomes most concrete. Decisions are evaluated where they originate rather than where their consequences accumulate. A sourcing decision that optimizes cost within procurement may introduce quality variability that manufacturing must absorb. A commercial timeline that satisfies revenue objectives may compress operational delivery beyond what the system can reliably sustain. A product specification may reflect sound engineering judgment while introducing integration requirements that fall between two teams whose formal accountability stops at their respective boundaries.

Inside each function accountability appears intact and outcomes look reasonable. Across the system accountability dissolves because outcomes increasingly reflect compounded interaction rather than discrete ownership. What is measured is the health of the boxes. What determines the outcome is the health of the connections between them.

The gap between what each function owned and what the integrated outcome required became measurable within one planning cycle. That held across every operating environment where I traced this pattern. Strategic intent exposes this most clearly because strategy requires translation across the most boundaries simultaneously. A directive issued at the center must travel across multiple domains before it becomes action. Each domain interprets it according to its own context, incentives, and operational constraints. Sales interprets a growth directive as expanded commercial commitments. Operations interprets it as increased throughput within existing capacity. Finance interprets it as margin discipline to preserve return on capital. Each interpretation is coherent within its own frame. When the organization attempts to execute the directive collectively, the divergence becomes visible because the underlying assumptions were never reconciled before work began.

What appears as execution failure is often the delayed recognition that intent changed meaning as it moved across boundaries because no mechanism existed to preserve it in transit.

You have seen this. The strategic initiative that produced three different operational realities from one leadership decision. The roadmap that finance, product, and sales each read differently, not because anyone misunderstood but because the same language carried different operational implications across the boundary. The divergence was structural and the conversation that followed was not.

Organizations rarely lack information about what their teams are doing. What they consistently lack is visibility into how meaning transforms as work crosses the boundaries between those teams. These interfaces do not appear on organizational charts or performance dashboards, yet they govern execution reliability more directly than any activity occurring inside the functions themselves. The most important determinant of execution reliability is the one that is structurally invisible in how most organizations measure themselves.

Once the organization is seen as a system rather than as a collection of functions, the governing question changes. The problem becomes how expectations retain their meaning, authority, and consequence as they travel across the system. Execution reliability depends on whether intent can survive those translations: whether authority arrives where decisions must be made, and whether commitments remain intact after they leave the room in which they were agreed.

The structural answer to that question has a specific requirement. A management system carries expectations reliably from origin to outcome only while the sequence connecting those two points remains protected. Financial conditions, operational constraints, and strategic preferences must influence decisions before commitments are made. Once commitments exist, the sequence through which they are delivered must be governed as a structural condition rather than renegotiated under internal pressure. The moment that sequence becomes discretionary, the chain through which expectations travel has already been broken, regardless of what the performance reports show.

This is where governance discipline enters as a structural mechanism rather than as a compliance function. When governance allows execution sequence to be rewritten after commitments exist, the system loses its authority over behavior; case-by-case discretion can resolve individual situations but cannot produce reliability at scale. It cannot make the organization's word mean something the market can count on.

What carries intent across those boundaries determines whether execution becomes a property of the system or remains dependent on the individuals currently compensating for its absence. Two organizations operating in the same market with comparable capability will diverge on this dimension. One builds the architecture. The other keeps building the people to compensate for not having it. The difference is not visible in any single quarter. It compounds in every one that follows.

CHAPTER 8
EXPECTATION TRANSMISSION: WHAT ACTUALLY CARRIES EXECUTION

THE MEDIUM

Expectations are the medium through which intent becomes execution. When that medium is never designed to preserve meaning, divergence appears across the organization even when every function is well led and every person is committed. Most organizations attribute the divergence to coordination complexity or uneven capability, but both point at people without reaching the structural condition producing the divergence. Expectations must travel through the organization to become results, and the system carrying them has not been built to preserve their meaning across the distance they must cross.

That distinction determines where corrective effort lands: one diagnosis directs investment toward people, the other toward the design of the system carrying the expectation. Organizations that fix the first without addressing the second spend years improving communication while the same structural condition continues generating the same coordination failures every planning cycle.

I encountered this directly in a commercial operation in South America. The organization had just completed a leadership meeting that, by every visible measure, had gone well. The strategy was clear, the commitments were named, and the follow-up documentation was thorough. I arrived several weeks later to find that the same strategic priority had produced three distinct operating realities. Sales had moved toward commercial volume, operations had moved toward delivery stability, and finance had moved toward margin protection. Each function had understood the direction and acted on it. None of them had arrived at the same place.

The COO I was working with had run that room correctly. None of it had survived the distance between the room and the execution layer. I spent two days inside the organization before the picture became clear. The people were capable and the room had been well run. What I found was something more structural. The expectation had depreciated in transit, and by the time it reached the people doing the work, it had been translated into three operating mandates with no mechanism for converging. The issue was what the expectation had become by the time it arrived.

This pattern persists because imprecision works under proximity. In smaller organizations shared context and continuous interaction compensate for weak encoding. Direction can be stated loosely and teams converge because everyone remains close enough to the source of the expectation to reconstruct its meaning in real time. As organizations scale, that proximity disappears and expectations must cross functions, hierarchies, and operating conditions that do not share the same context as the point of origin. When expectations are not engineered to survive that journey, interpretation replaces transmission. The resulting pattern is consistent: outcomes remain reliable near the center where expectations originate and progressively variable at the edges where expectations must be interpreted.

Leaders often conclude that execution quality declines with distance because capability declines with distance. The actual variable is the fidelity of the medium carrying the expectation. People operating at the edges are rarely less capable than those at the center. They are executing against a signal that has lost operational precision at every boundary it crossed. Their work therefore includes both execution and the reconstruction of meaning that should have arrived intact. That extra effort is invisible in any performance metric. It shows up only in the increasing volume of managerial labor required to keep the work coherent.

Wherever this condition persisted past the point of first visibility, the response followed the same pattern: add oversight, increase communication, run more alignment sessions. Each measure provided temporary relief because none addressed the transmission design. The same interpretation gap reappeared in the next planning cycle with different people having the same conversation. Across three continents, in industries as different as consumer goods and financial services, the pattern did not vary by sector or by the quality of the people involved. The transmission system was never designed, the repair mechanisms multiplied around its absence, and the gap remained.

Organizations compensate for expectation depreciation by expanding interpretive labor, and they do so without recognizing what they are compensating for. Managers clarify meaning through meetings and calls. Teams build private translation documents that convert leadership language into operating tasks. Regional leaders seek confirmation before acting because the policy statements they receive lack the precision required to govern the conditions they face. Interpretation accumulates as managerial labor while the loss of transmission fidelity that created the labor stays invisible.

That normalization is where the problem compounds. The degradation that follows is uneven rather than uniform, and that unevenness is diagnostic. If the problem were capability, weaker teams would consistently underperform. If the problem were alignment, divergence would appear in predictable directions. When the same directive produces excellent results in one area and costly variance in another with no consistent pattern, the variable is the medium carrying the expectation. Uneven degradation is the signature of transmission failure.

What I found underneath the coordination complexity was always the same thing: a transmission system that was never built. Every condition examined in Part II traces back to this same structural cause. Leadership dependency takes hold when expectations require repeated clarification from their origin. The competence trap deepens when skilled individuals repeatedly reconstruct meaning that should have been encoded structurally. The heroism cycle runs when leaders intervene to reconcile interpretations that diverged earlier in the execution chain. Alignment theater sustains when organizations restore coherence through conversation rather than through the design of the medium carrying expectations forward. All four are symptoms of expectation depreciation in transit.

Most organizations attempt to manage this depreciation through meetings, updates, alignment sessions, and leadership involvement. These mechanisms restore coherence temporarily by bringing people closer to the source of the expectation. They are events through which organizations periodically repair the signal when no stable medium exists to carry it reliably.

Events restore proximity. Systems preserve meaning.

At scale, execution requires the latter. Expectations must be treated not as statements of direction but as engineered units of operational meaning capable of surviving distance, time, and competing local incentives without requiring continued interpretation from the individual who issued them. The sequence through which intent becomes execution must remain intact across the organization.

The sequence is straightforward: intent becomes expectations, expectations enter transmission, and transmission must preserve meaning so that translation into local action remains consistent with the original intent. That translation produces execution, and execution produces results. When the transmission stage fails, every subsequent stage reorganizes around interpretation rather than the original expectation. I have not seen an exception to this sequence in thirty years across operating environments with very different cultures, languages, and organizational models. The failure mode changes in name but the mechanism holds every time.

When this condition is resolved, the shift shows within one or two planning cycles. The volume of clarification meetings dropped because the expectations arriving at the execution layer no longer required clarification to hold. Leaders whose weeks had been dominated by interpretive labor found their attention available for work only they could do. The same teams that had been producing variable results in one context and reliable results in another began producing reliable results throughout because the variable had been addressed.

The clarification work disappears because the expectation was designed to not need it. Organizations that resolve this condition treat expectations as elements of a transmission system rather than as statements issued during meetings. The expectation must be encoded with enough structural clarity that its meaning survives the boundaries it must cross. Transmission becomes a designed property of the operating system rather than an informal process sustained through clarification and oversight.

Where this precision matters most is at the interfaces where work changes hands. Strategy translating into budgets. Budgets into operating plans. Operating plans into daily decisions. Each boundary requires expectations that retain operational meaning without requiring interpretation from the point of origin. The organizations that design this system gain execution reliability. The signal governing action remains stable across the system in a way that effort alone cannot produce.

Expectations always travel through the organization. The question is how they must be encoded before they enter the system so their meaning survives every boundary they must cross. You know which of these two organizations you are in. The more useful question is whether the design decision that separates them can still be made before scale makes the cost visible. The organizations that have answered that question do not look more aligned than the ones that have not. They look more finished and their commitments arrive intact. Their teams work on execution rather than on reconstruction. One organization keeps rebuilding alignment because the medium carrying its expectations keeps losing what it was given. The other builds the medium once and compounds on it. The difference between them is a design decision, and it sits at the boundary where the expectation first leaves the room.

CHAPTER 9
THE INTERFACE SYSTEM: HOW THE ORGANIZATION ACTUALLY OPERATES

THE BOUNDARY

Execution occurs horizontally. Commitments move across the interfaces connecting functions into a working system. Those crossings are where meaning either survives translation or begins to degrade. They appear on no organizational chart, sit inside no function's domain, and belong to no named owner.

I have been in this conversation more times than I can count. A COO traces a quarterly variance backward through otherwise competent functions and arrives at a space no one designed. Sales exceeded its pipeline target. Operations met its throughput metrics. Finance closed the books within cycle. Each function performed within its expected range. The integrated result missed by a margin that no single function can explain or claim.

The trace reveals why. A commercial commitment was priced using cost assumptions that procurement had already revised. A delivery timeline was confirmed against a production schedule that had shifted two weeks earlier without triggering a revalidation. An inventory position that appeared sufficient within the warehouse function proved inadequate at the system level because two product lines were drawing from the same buffer without either team recognizing the other's demand. The people involved are capable and the processes inside the functions are sound. The failure sits at the boundary where work changes hands.

Senior leaders instinctively read the enterprise vertically because hierarchy governs authority, escalation, and accountability. Budgets are allocated to functions. Performance is reviewed within functions. Improvement initiatives are assigned to the leaders responsible for those domains. The interpretation that results appear to be the sum of functional performance holds only when work stays inside the boxes. Once execution requires commitments to travel across specialization, time, and operational distance, outcomes depend on what happens at the boundaries where one function's output becomes another's input. Functions can perform competently in isolation while integration fails at the boundary where their activities must converge. The failure is architectural. It sits in the space between the functions, at the point of crossing, where no function holds design authority and no performance metric reaches.

While In conversation with COOs across multiple industries and operating environments.a consistent pattern emerges. The variance is explained in functional terms. The actual cause sits at a boundary between functions. The review system is not designed to see that boundary, so the explanation stays accurate within what the system can measure and wrong about what the system needs to correct.

You know this boundary. You have stood at it or you have sent work across it and watched it return changed. The interface is the specific place in your operating structure where execution either holds its meaning or begins to fragment. When those boundaries are unmanaged, translation loss accumulates between otherwise capable units in a pattern that is entirely predictable once you know what to look for.

I have seen a commercial organization operating across six countries hold consistent revenue performance at the center while losing margin systematically at the edges for three consecutive quarters. The diagnosis inside each country was execution quality. The actual variable, as I found when I traced the pattern backward, was the boundary between regional commercial decisions and central supply allocation. Nobody owned that crossing. Every function that touched it owned only one side of it.

A supply chain director reduces buffer inventory to improve holding costs. The savings appear in her function's P&L while the stockout risk materializes in commercial results two months later. A product manager finalizes a specification that satisfies engineering standards while creating a procurement dependency that manufacturing discovers only during assembly. A regional sales director closes a contract within his margin authority while committing a delivery schedule that logistics can meet only by diverting capacity from another region. Each decision is competent within the function that made it. The cost appears at the boundary the decision-maker could not see and did not own.

Organizations interpret these events as coordination failures requiring better communication. They are architectural failures requiring governed interfaces. The distinction matters because the response to a coordination failure is more conversation, and more conversation does not govern a boundary. It temporarily bridges one.

When interfaces are not designed, accountability becomes distorted in a specific way. Leaders are held responsible for outcomes that no single function can control end to end. Execution owners compensate by negotiating scope informally, absorbing variance locally, or reinterpreting commitments to keep delivery moving. Performance reviews stay anchored to activities inside functions because those activities are measurable and assignable. Failure originates in the space between them, where coordination work exists but is structurally invisible. The result is an accountability system capable of explaining misses without preventing them. Post-incident reviews produce findings within functions because measurement systems reach those locations. The actual cause often sits at a boundary where meaning changed during transmission, at a crossing that appears on no organizational chart and inside no accountability model.

The earliest economic signature of unmanaged interfaces is time loss, not visible failure. Work waits at boundaries for clarification, sequencing decisions, reconciliation of assumptions, or re-commitment of scope. These delays normalize within the operating rhythm and are absorbed as the cost of complexity. Capital follows. Buffers appear to compensate for uncertainty at crossings. Duplicate verification steps emerge in adjacent teams. Contingency capacity is inserted to protect against unpredictable demand from neighboring functions.

The people who are best at managing these crossings eventually leave. Sustaining perpetual negotiation across boundaries that should have been governed is a specific kind of exhaustion, different from the exhaustion of hard work. It is the exhaustion of compensating continuously for a structural condition that no one is addressing, because the compensation keeps working well enough to make addressing it feel unnecessary. When those people leave, the organization discovers that what it thought was a process was actually a person.

The shift, when this condition gets resolved, has the same character every time. The boundaries stopped requiring continuous negotiation because the expectations arriving at them were encoded to survive the crossing without reconstruction. The boundary that had been consuming leadership attention stopped consuming it. Not because the people changed, but because the architecture replaced the negotiation.

The organization's operating system is its interface topology: the pattern of crossings where work changes form, authority transfers, and expectations must survive translation in order for execution to proceed. That system is the one that actually governs whether work moves coherently or stalls, whether meaning survives or degrades, and it appears on no organizational chart.

Once those crossings are governed by design, direction travels farther without distortion. Local optimization occurs without destabilizing the system. Execution becomes less dependent on the individuals standing at the boundary and more dependent on the architecture governing how work moves through them.

Building that architecture requires naming what the governed interfaces must produce and making that requirement a structural property of how expectations are encoded before they enter the crossing. These three governing conditions: sequence, load, and cadence, form what I have come to describe as the Strategic Management Operating System: SMOS. Its purpose is to ensure that once expectations are defined and contracted, they move through the organization without losing sequence, capacity, or validity.

Architecture explains how the organization is built. SMOS governs how execution moves within it.

It does not override a culture built on fear or bad faith, but it removes the structural conditions that make fear and bad faith the rational choice.

Execution at scale is governed by three conditions that clarity alone cannot supply, regardless of how precisely expectations are encoded. These three conditions are preventive rather than corrective. They stop the problem from emerging rather than responding after it has appeared. Neither can substitute for the other. What remains for leadership is the governance of the conditions under which activity remains valid, whether the direction the system is advancing still warrants the effort sustaining it, whether the language encoding expectations retains the precision architecture requires.

The COO who traced the quarterly variance backward through otherwise competent functions has now reached the point where the underlying structure is visible. The organization's execution depends on expectation fidelity in transit, and its reliability is determined at the interfaces where commitments change hands. The architecture of execution must be built at those interfaces, with the instruments that allow it to carry work without requiring someone to stand at the boundary and negotiate each crossing. That is the transition from architecture to orchestration, and it is where Part IV begins.

PART FOUR

FROM ACTION TO ORCHESTRATION

CHAPTER 10
WHEN ARCHITECTURE IS NO LONGER ENOUGH

THE SHIFT

The architecture is now complete: interfaces between functions are governed, expectations are encoded with enough precision to survive transit across boundaries, and accountability moves with the work rather than returning to the center for resolution.

The system carries arrangement reliably. It does not carry motion.

That single distinction marks the limit of architecture. The system organizes work in the correct arrangement and maintains structural coherence across functions. It does not generate forward motion for strategic or cross-functional initiatives that must advance through changing conditions. Those initiatives still require the leader personally to supply momentum: re-sequencing priorities when conditions shift, authorizing movement when dependencies collide, reconciling interference when functions optimize locally. Routine work continued without interruption because the structure holds it in place. Strategic motion stops because the advancement of those initiatives was never transferred into the system's regulatory logic.

Most leaders who reach this point interpret the stall as evidence that the architectural work was incomplete. They respond by adding more structure or more personal involvement. That response directs corrective effort toward the wrong layer, and the condition remains.

The architecture governs arrangement. Orchestration governs motion, and the two are not the same. Organizations that recognize the distinction early install the instruments that allow execution to advance independently. Those that do not remain dependent on the continued availability of the leader who built the first layer.

This threshold emerged in a commercial operation I led across several markets. The business had grown rapidly, and I had invested eighteen months building the operating architecture the scale required. Interfaces were defined and governed, expectations were encoded precisely enough to hold their meaning across boundaries, and accountability moved with the work rather than returning to the center for resolution. The architecture held everything it had been designed to hold.

Then I stepped away for three weeks, the first time in four years. Operational cadence continued without interruption. Governed interfaces allowed activity to move through known paths. Encoded expectations allowed decisions to resolve locally. Distributed authority allowed routine work to proceed without escalation. All of that held.

The strategic initiatives stalled. By day eight, a commercial expansion that had been advancing every week reached a sequencing decision and stopped. Nobody escalated it, because the system had no path for escalation, because the decision required weighing two competing strategic priorities, and that judgment had always lived with me. By day eleven, a product initiative reached a resource allocation question where both teams were accountable, both knew what was needed, and neither had the authority to resolve the trade-off independently. At the end of week two, a market entry plan required re-authorization because a cost assumption had shifted. There was no cadence governing when re-authorization was required, so the work waited. Three initiatives, three different reasons, the same underlying cause: I had organized the work without transferring the logic that would allow it to move without me present.

Their advancement had never been transferred into the system's regulatory logic. They moved when I moved them. They paused when I was unavailable. The architecture had organized the work without giving the work the capacity to move on its own.

As this condition persists, the organization adapts to it in ways that reinforce it. Commitments calibrate to perceived access rather than governed sequence. Priorities synchronize to urgency signals rather than structural logic. Teams become skilled at managing access to leadership attention, reading which initiatives are being watched closely and which can wait. Advancement depends on the presence of the individual who can authorize movement when the system itself carries no mechanism to authorize it. Initiatives advance in bursts when attention concentrates and stall when attention shifts.

You know this specific oscillation. The planning cycle that produces excellent plans whose execution depends entirely on whether the leader who shaped them continues supplying the momentum that converts plan into motion. The gradual realization, accumulating over months, that the system runs efficiently yet advances only when someone is actively pushing it forward.

The economic cost of this condition accumulates in forms that structural design was meant to eliminate. In my experience the leader who carries sequencing work spends 30 to 40 percent of their available week on motion management rather than direction. That portion is not discretionary; it is the minimum required to keep the strategic layer advancing. Every hour spent resequencing commitments, authorizing movement, and reconciling interference comes directly from external sensing, strategic evaluation, and the judgment work that only leadership altitude can perform. The work that leadership should be doing recedes. The work that the system should be doing expands to fill the space.

When the leader is the authorization mechanism, strategic priorities advance in the order that leadership attention reaches them, not in the order that causal logic requires. A high-value initiative that depends on decisions the leader has not yet reached waits behind a lower-value one the leader happened to review first. The system produces results ordered by proximity to the leader's calendar rather than by the organization's strategic logic. Two planning cycles in the same operation made the pattern specific enough to trace. The architecture was sound. The sequencing that governed which work advanced reflected nothing more than what I had last touched, and the organization had no mechanism to correct it in my absence.

The third cost is the deepest. The organization never develops the capacity to govern its own motion. Each cycle the leader carries the same sequencing work, and each cycle the organization finishes exactly as dependent as when it began. The structural improvement that would eliminate the dependency is perpetually displaced by the operational carrying that prevents the dependency from becoming visible. Capital is consumed through repeated initiative launches that exceed the system's capacity to absorb them under stable conditions. Effort cycles between surge and recovery rather than compounding into steady throughput. Optionality narrows because leadership attention is spent preserving momentum rather than shaping future conditions.

Two planning cycles in the same commercial operation produced a pattern specific enough to trace with precision. In the first cycle, three initiatives were advancing simultaneously. One was a market expansion that required commercial and operational decisions to move in a fixed sequence. The second was a product development program whose resource requirements overlapped with the first. The third was a distribution partnership that could only close after the market expansion had established its initial foothold. None of this dependency structure had been mapped before execution began.

By the end of the first cycle, the market expansion had advanced because it held my attention most often. The product development program had reached a resourcing decision and stopped there, not because the decision was difficult but because no one in the system had the authority to make it without my involvement, and my involvement was occupied elsewhere. The distribution partnership had not moved at all. Its entry condition, the foothold the market expansion was supposed to establish, had not yet been met, and nothing in the system signaled that the partnership was waiting for something the other initiative had not yet produced.

In the second cycle the pattern repeated with different initiatives in the same structural positions. What the two cycles revealed was not a capability problem or a resourcing problem. They revealed that the sequencing mechanism was my calendar, and my calendar had no logic in it that corresponded to the causal dependencies governing what the system actually needed to advance. The organization was not failing to execute. It was executing in the wrong order, every cycle, without any instrument to detect it.

That is the third cost made concrete: an organization that cannot govern its own sequence cannot compound. It can only repeat.

The organization has reached the limit of what architecture alone can govern. The instruments that allow work to carry itself across boundaries and through time have not yet been installed. That is the transition this chapter marks.

The chapters that follow install the three governing instruments that make motion structural rather than personal.

CHAPTER 11
SEQUENCE AS SYSTEM

THE ORDER

Orchestration begins where architecture ends. The interfaces are now governed, the expectations encoded, and accountability placed with the work itself. What remains unresolved is the order in which new commitments are permitted to enter motion. That single variable decides whether effort compounds into coherent progress or fragments into interference.

Without governed sequence, even well-designed initiatives collide at the points where their dependencies intersect. The system absorbs the resulting friction through coordination and personal intervention, but the underlying condition stays unchanged. The architecture holds the arrangement; it does not govern the timing of entry.

Organizations paid this collision tax across every market and operating environment where sequence was absent. The pattern is identical once the surface noise is removed.

I encountered this pattern in an operating environment where a vice president coordinating several strategic initiatives faced exactly this condition. Every individual program looked sound and the integrated result was deteriorating. She was overseeing three well-designed programs, each with clear objectives, capable teams, and sufficient resources. Each one, reviewed on its own terms, was viable. The problem surfaced when all three entered motion at the same time. She spent more time reconciling interference between the three initiatives than advancing any of them. Each required inputs, decisions, or capacity that overlapped with the others. Because those dependencies had not been stabilized before execution began, teams encountered conflicts only after work was already underway. Priorities were renegotiated repeatedly as resources shifted between initiatives and each team discovered what the others required. Decisions were revisited for a consistent reason: they had been made outside the order required for them to hold.

Execution had begun before the system was ready to absorb it, and the capability of the people inside it could not carry what the sequencing had failed to establish.

The change was gradual enough that no one scheduled it. It became visible in retrospect only after someone had already absorbed the coordination tax long enough to recognize the shape of it.

You have managed a version of this. The Monday morning where several initiatives have stalled at different gates, each waiting for the same authorization, all drawing from the same finite hours. The planning cycle where re-sequencing the same priorities for the third time in three weeks has nothing to do with anything strategic changing and everything to do with the fact that nothing in the system has ever determined the order in which work should move. That exhaustion has a specific character. It belongs to the repeated management of consequences a governed system would have prevented.

When sequence is absent, organizations compensate through coordination. Meetings multiply and communication intensifies as leaders intervene to realign priorities and resolve conflicts while execution progresses. The organization reads this activity as management, though the two operate differently. Management prevents the problem from arising. Recovery addresses it after it has arrived, and an organization in permanent recovery builds skill at the wrong activity.

Sequence governs causality. Speed follows from order. Accelerating work that entered the system before the conditions to sustain it were in place produces interference, not throughput. Work must enter motion only after the conditions required to sustain it have been established. Decisions must precede the actions they authorize. Dependencies must be resolved before they are encountered. Capacity must be available before it is consumed. When those conditions hold, each step in the execution chain has stable ground beneath it. When they are absent, execution fragments.

The cost of fragmentation is rarely visible at the level of individual initiatives. Each project continues advancing and producing partial results that appear valid in isolation. The cost appears at the system level, where interference reduces the rate at which outcomes can be integrated into coherent progress. The collision tax is the cost of doing things in the wrong order, and organizations pay it every time a commitment enters motion before the conditions required to sustain it have been met.

Past the point of first recognition, the response is always the same: add resources, increase oversight, accelerate activity. Each measure increased concurrency without addressing the ordering condition generating the interference, and as more work entered the system, more interference followed. The decisions being made were structurally correct and causally wrong, made in the right direction, in the wrong order.

The outcome is the same every time this response runs its course. The concurrency level rose, the interference grew, and the leaders who had added resources found themselves managing a more expensive version of the original condition rather than a different one.

The governing response to the collision tax is counterintuitive because it looks like restraint. Sequence governs the order in which work is allowed to begin, and this governance enables throughput rather than constraining it. When initiatives enter motion in the correct order, outputs from one become stable inputs for the next. Decisions remain valid because the premises authorizing them have not expired. Teams advance without renegotiating priorities because those priorities were established before execution began, and the accumulation of completed work creates absorptive capacity for the work that follows.

The absence of sequence forces the organization into a reactive posture. Work begins before it is ready, the system spends energy resolving conflicts rather than advancing outcomes, and teams build skill at managing interference rather than at completing work. Leaders build skill at re-sequencing priorities rather than at governing the conditions that would make re-sequencing structurally unnecessary. The organization becomes increasingly proficient at a problem it could have designed out of existence.

When sequence governs the order in which work enters motion, the conflicts that consumed coordination capacity never materialize, because the work that would have generated them waits at the release gate until the conditions required to sustain it are in place. The need for intervention declines because the design has removed the source of the problems. Prevention replaces speed of recovery as the measure of a well-governed system.

The shift took hold in a commercial operation I was responsible for across several markets. Before governed sequence was installed, the weekly operating rhythm was dominated by re-sequencing conversations, the same priorities revisited for the third or fourth time because nothing structural had determined the order in which they should move. After it was installed, those conversations stopped. The work the re-sequencing had been doing moved into the system's release logic, and the leadership time that had been consumed by interference management freed for the decisions the system cannot make on its own. The shift was visible within one planning cycle. What had taken three or four meetings of re-sequencing conversations to resolve each cycle now moved through the system without requiring a room or a decision from above to authorize it.

Once this discipline is installed, the calendar of the people responsible for sequencing empties of the work the release logic now carries. The re-sequencing meetings that had filled Monday mornings stopped arising. The resource conflicts that had produced those meetings did not migrate elsewhere. They stopped because the work that would have generated them was waiting at the release gate rather than already in motion. Sequence had made the problem structurally impossible rather than personally managed.

The organization that governs sequence does work that builds on itself, in an order that allows each completed commitment to strengthen the foundation for what follows. It approves the work it will finish rather than the work it intends to start. It governs the entry point for commitments rather than responding to the interference they generate once already in motion.

The organization that has not yet installed this instrument manages sequence through the continuous availability of people capable of re-sequencing priorities under pressure and reconciling the interference that unmanaged concurrency produces. When those people are present, execution continues. When their attention shifts, the system discovers that it has been operating without the structural logic they were substituting for.

Sequence is the first instrument of orchestration because it determines whether the system operates through accumulation or interference. The organizations that install it correctly move faster by finishing more, committing only to the work the system can carry to completion in the correct causal order.

The difference between activity and progress is entirely a function of order.

CHAPTER 12
LOAD AS LATENT CONSTRAINT

THE CAPACITY

Sequence now governs the order in which commitments are permitted to enter motion. The remaining question is whether the system possesses the absorptive space required to receive that work without degrading the commitments already underway. Load is the instrument that answers this question. With interfaces governed and expectations encoded, the architecture has already placed accountability where it belongs. Sequence directs the causal order while load determines the volume the system can carry at any one time, and the two conditions are interdependent. Without the second, the first loses its power to compound.

Organizations crossed this threshold in commercial operations and fulfillment networks across multiple markets, always the same way. The same threshold appears across every operating environment where load goes ungoverned. The breach always arrived gradually enough that the static indicators stayed sound while the system's integrative capacity was already exhausted. A chief operating officer managing a fulfillment network watched the operation cross its absorption threshold without any instrument capable of detecting it. At lower utilization levels, delivery reliability remained stable and the network absorbed incremental demand without visible strain. As volume increased, utilization rose toward what the leadership team interpreted as improved efficiency. The static indicators still appeared sound: staffing levels were intact, budgets held, and workflows remained formally unchanged. Within three quarters, on-time delivery had fallen, escalation volume had doubled, and throughput had declined despite higher activity levels across the network. Longer hours produced more coordination meetings, while the underlying cause remained invisible: the system had exceeded its absorptive capacity, yet no structural signal had warned anyone that the ceiling had been breached.

The leadership team responded with the tools they understood. They added resources, accelerated schedules, and intensified oversight. Each measure increased concurrency without addressing the volume condition that had already been violated, and the interference grew. The very capability that had once sustained performance now became the mechanism that concealed the breach. Teams worked harder and coordination multiplied. Results continued to slip because the system had been asked to carry more than it could sustain without degradation. This outcome was the mechanical consequence of load beyond absorptive capacity.

The organization that runs this response pattern emerges more capable at triage and less capable at prevention than it was before the breach. That trade-off compounds with each cycle. The capacity for clear planning that the organization had once held had been replaced by the capacity to manage the consequences of not planning clearly enough.

You know this quarter. The quarter when every function reported green yet the integrated result slipped. The planning session where six new initiatives were approved because each one looked reasonable in isolation, yet the system had no remaining capacity to absorb them all. The exhaustion that followed was not the exhaustion of hard work but the exhaustion of perpetual triage. Leaders spent their attention arbitrating between commitments that should never have entered simultaneous motion. You saw the same faces in back-to-back meetings. Each person defended why their priority could not wait. Each one drew from the same finite pool of engineering hours, capital budget, and management focus. The calendar filled with arbitration sessions that produced temporary relief but never addressed the root condition, and the organization appeared busy and responsive while progress slowed because the system was being asked to hold more than its design allowed.

When load is ungoverned, organizations compensate through arbitration. Meetings multiply, decisions are revisited as leaders intervene to reconcile competing claims on finite capacity, and teams learn to escalate early rather than commit to timelines they cannot protect. The organization reads this activity as management, though the two operate differently, since management prevents the problem from arising while recovery addresses it after it has arrived. An organization in permanent recovery builds skill at the wrong activity. They negotiate for resources rather than execute within them. They defend their slice of capacity rather than contribute to the overall flow. Leaders become proficient at triage rather than at design. The system learns to survive on constant intervention instead of operating within governed limits.

Once the load condition is named, the escalation patterns become entirely predictable. This behavior embed itself across industries and operating environments, the rationality of it is always the same. The people inside the system were not behaving badly. They were behaving correctly given what the system had taught them to expect.

Load governs capacity. When the volume of concurrent work remains within the system's absorptive ceiling, each commitment advances without degrading the others. Outputs from one initiative remain stable inputs for the next. Teams move forward without renegotiating resources because those resources were never over-allocated. The system compounds rather than fragments. Delivery reliability stabilizes because the work never exceeds what the network can carry to completion. Strategic initiatives complete on schedule because capacity was protected before it was consumed. Resource allocation decisions hold across quarters because the ceiling was respected from the moment of release.

The shift took hold in the same fulfillment network once the absorption ceiling was installed. Before it existed, weekly operating rhythms were dominated by triage conversations. The same resource conflicts were revisited because nothing structural had ever defined the volume the system could carry. Once the ceiling was in place, those conversations disappeared. The work the triage had been doing moved into the system's release logic. The leadership time that had been consumed by interference management became available for what only the governing edge can answer. The change showed up within one cycle. On-time delivery recovered to previous levels while volume increased. Escalation traffic declined because the conditions that generated escalation had been removed. Teams reported higher confidence in their ability to deliver because they knew the system would not ask them to carry more than it could sustain.

The organization that governs load commits only to what it can carry to completion. It maintains the ceiling that prevents interference from arising. Decision fatigue that the organization had attributed to cultural problems reveals itself as the mechanical consequence of load beyond absorptive capacity. Leadership attention that had been consumed by throughput arbitration becomes available for the questions only the governing edge can answer. Capacity, properly understood, is what the system can absorb to completion without degrading the flow already in motion.

Sequence governs whether work enters in the right order. Load governs whether the system can hold the volume now inside it. Together they determine whether the work that enters the system advances coherently. Neither yet governs how long commitments retain their authority once they are already moving. A system can release work in the correct order and within its absorptive capacity and still lose coherence if commitments remain active after the assumptions that authorized them have expired. That temporal condition is what the third governing instrument addresses. Where both instruments operated together, the coherence they produced was qualitatively different from what either produced alone.

To understand the full weight of load as a latent constraint, consider how it operates across different layers of the organization. At the operational level, load determines whether production schedules remain valid or collapse under overlapping demands. In one manufacturing network I led, we tracked buffer utilization across three plants. When load remained within the governed ceiling, each plant maintained its promised lead times and quality standards. When load exceeded the ceiling, even by fifteen percent, the buffers emptied faster than replenishment cycles could restore them. The result was not a single failure but a cascading series of delays that affected every downstream customer commitment. The teams were competent, the equipment was reliable, and the processes were documented. The system simply lacked the structural limit that would have prevented the overload.

At the strategic level, load determines whether initiatives reinforce one another or compete for the same scarce attention. I observed this in a regional expansion program across Southeast Asia. Three market entries were approved in rapid succession because each appeared attractive on its own merits. The combined load on the shared supply chain, talent pool, and leadership bandwidth exceeded what the organization could sustain. Within six months, two of the entries were delayed, one was scaled back, and the third required emergency intervention to avoid failure. The root cause was not poor strategy or weak execution but the absence of a governed absorption ceiling that would have forced sequencing or deferral until capacity caught up.

The cost of ungoverned load extends beyond immediate results. It erodes trust in the planning process itself. Teams learn that commitments made at the top are subject to later arbitration, so they build contingency into every forecast. Leaders learn that approval does not guarantee delivery, so they hesitate to commit resources to new work. The organization develops a culture of cautious over-promising followed by negotiated under-delivery. This culture formed in organizations that had once been decisive and confident, always within one or two planning cycles of the first ungoverned overload. The shift was not slow; it arrived at the planning table within one or two cycles and did not leave. None of this behavior is irrational, because it is the rational response to a system that has never defined its own capacity limits.

When load is governed, the opposite dynamic emerges. Teams plan with confidence because they know the system will protect their capacity. Leaders approve work with clarity because the ceiling has already been respected. The organization builds skill at finishing rather than starting. Progress becomes visible and predictable because the work that enters the system is the work the system can carry to completion. This instrument does not reduce ambition but channels it into sustainable execution. The organization that respects its absorption ceiling moves faster because it avoids the recovery cycles that consume more time than the original work itself. It compounds capability because completed commitments create the foundation for the next wave of growth. It preserves leadership bandwidth for the work that truly requires judgment rather than arbitration.

Where the absorption ceiling was installed, the organizations that built it and the ones that did not diverged in a specific and measurable way. The one operating within governed load limits completed more, arbitrated less, and compounded its capacity across cycles, while the one carrying ungoverned load kept resetting.

The difference is structural. One organization operates as a collection of capable functions that must be constantly reconciled at the center. The other operates as an integrated system whose capacity limits are known and respected before work is released. The first depends on the continuous availability of people who can arbitrate interference. The second depends on the design that prevents interference from arising.

Load as latent constraint is therefore not a limitation on growth. It is the condition that makes sustained growth possible. When the system knows what it can carry, it carries it reliably. When leadership governs volume rather than arbitrating overload, attention returns to direction, expectation fidelity, and system design. The organization no longer pays the hidden tax of perpetual triage. It invests that capacity in the work that builds competitive advantage.

The same outcome appeared within two planning cycles, every operation where I installed this instrument. Delivery reliability improved and strategic completion rates rose. Leadership meetings shortened because the agenda no longer included arbitration of capacity conflicts. The system became self-regulating in the dimension of volume, freeing leadership to focus on the dimensions that remain irreducibly human.

CHAPTER 13
CADENCE: THE LIFESPAN OF AUTHORIZATION

THE RENEWAL

Sequence and load now operate together. Work enters in the correct causal order and remains within the system's absorptive capacity. What remains unresolved is the temporal condition: how long any commitment remains valid once it is already moving. Authorization does not last indefinitely. The conditions that justified the original decision change, yet without a governed renewal rhythm the commitment continues to consume resources and attention as though those conditions still hold. The system carries work that no longer aligns with reality, and the misalignment accumulates until results expose it.

Organizations paid this temporal tax across commercial operations in the Americas and Asia, the mechanism was identical in each. The pattern is consistent once the surface indicators are stripped away. A commercial director overseeing channel strategy in a high-volume protein business authorized a major market expansion program with clear assumptions about customer demand, supply chain stability, and competitive positioning. The initiative entered motion in the correct sequence and within the system's absorption ceiling. For the first two quarters the program advanced on plan. By the third quarter the assumptions that had authorized it had shifted: demand softened in one key segment, a new competitor entered with a lower-cost offering, and supply chain costs rose beyond the original forecast. The program continued consuming budget and management attention because no structural mechanism existed to retire or reauthorize it. The team was executing yesterday's decision with today's resources, and the misalignment was invisible at the individual initiative level. Only at the integrated result did the drag become measurable.

The leadership response followed the familiar pattern: additional analysis was commissioned, status reviews were lengthened, and trade-off decisions were escalated to the executive level. Each step consumed more time and produced more documentation, yet the underlying condition remained. The escalation produced documentation and deferred the decision rather than reaching it. That held every time. The authorization had expired without a governed point of renewal or retirement, and the organization was investing in work whose original justification no longer existed.

The initiative that still appears on every status report months after its original justification has expired. The quarterly review where the team defends continued investment in a program whose assumptions no longer hold, yet no one can point to the moment when the authorization lapsed. The exhaustion that follows is specific: it belongs to the perpetual revalidation of decisions that should have been retired or renewed on schedule. You recognize the meeting where the same data is reviewed for the fourth time, the same trade-offs debated, the same request for more time to assess the situation. The calendar fills with revalidation sessions that produce temporary alignment but never address the root condition. The organization appears diligent and data-driven, yet strategic resources continue to flow toward work that has lost its relevance.

When cadence is absent, organizations compensate through re-authorization. Meetings multiply and decisions are revisited as leaders intervene to determine whether yesterday's commitments still make sense. The organization reads this activity as management, though the two operate differently, since management prevents the problem from arising while recovery addresses it after it has arrived. Teams learn to defend sunk costs rather than challenge outdated assumptions. Leaders become proficient at perpetual revalidation rather than at directional judgment. The system learns to survive on constant intervention instead of operating within a governed temporal rhythm. The revalidation meetings that multiplied were always a symptom of the same absence: no instrument governed when a commitment expired and no mechanism forced the question of whether it should be renewed.

Cadence governs the lifespan of authorization. When commitments are reviewed and explicitly renewed or retired at predictable intervals, every active initiative remains aligned with current conditions. The system carries only work that continues to warrant the effort sustaining it, and teams advance without the drag of outdated authorization holding resources against work that no longer earns them. Strategic resources flow toward opportunities that remain valid rather than toward legacy decisions that have expired. Each time I have seen a renewal rhythm installed, that flow reversed within one cycle and stayed reversed.

This shift takes hold in the same channel strategy program once the renewal rhythm was installed. Before it existed, quarterly reviews were dominated by revalidation conversations. The revalidation meetings that had dominated those cycles simply stopped arising. The work the revalidation had been doing moved into the system's renewal logic, and the leadership time that had been consumed by perpetual re-authorization freed for the decisions the system cannot make on its own. One planning cycle was enough to see it. The expansion program was formally retired at the next renewal gate because its assumptions no longer held. Resources were reallocated to a new opportunity that aligned with current market conditions. Delivery timelines stabilized because the system no longer carried the drag of expired commitments. The organization moved faster because it stopped investing in work that had lost its authority.

The governing response to temporal drift is counterintuitive because it looks like periodic interruption. Cadence forces renewal or retirement.

Effort compounds rather than cycles between surge and recovery. it is where the formulation first earns its place. The organization that governs cadence completes the governing set. Sequence prevents causal interference. Load prevents capacity interference. Cadence prevents temporal interference. Together they convert execution from a continuous exercise in recovery into a governed flow that compounds without constant intervention.

To appreciate the full power of cadence, consider how it operates across different time horizons. At the operational level, cadence determines whether weekly priorities remain valid or drift into irrelevance. In a business I led across Latin America, we established monthly renewal gates for all channel commitments. Before the rhythm existed, quarterly plans were set and then ignored as market conditions changed. Teams continued executing against assumptions that had become obsolete within weeks. After the renewal gates were installed, each commitment was explicitly reviewed against current data. Those that no longer justified the resources were retired. Those that remained valid were renewed with updated parameters. The result was not more bureaucracy but less waste. Resources flowed to live opportunities rather than to legacy plans.

At the strategic level, cadence determines whether multi-year initiatives retain their legitimacy or become structural debt. I observed this in a capacity expansion program spanning three countries. The original authorization rested on demand forecasts and cost assumptions that proved accurate for the first eighteen months. By month twenty-four, competitive dynamics had shifted and raw material costs had risen beyond the break-even threshold. Without cadence, the project continued consuming capital because no structural point existed to force re-evaluation. With cadence in place, the renewal gate at month twenty-four triggered an explicit decision: retire the expansion or revise its scope and funding. The organization chose revision, protected its capital, and redirected resources to a higher-return opportunity. The decision was difficult in the moment yet preserved the system's overall health.

The cost of ungoverned cadence extends beyond immediate financial results, eroding confidence in strategic planning itself. Teams learn that long-term commitments are subject to silent expiration, so they build buffers into every forecast. Leaders learn that authorization granted today may become a liability tomorrow, so they hesitate to commit resources to ambitious work. The organization develops a culture of cautious incrementalism followed by periodic resets. Multi-year programs showed this most clearly, assumptions had shifted within the first year while the commitment carried forward undisturbed, and the culture adjusted to the gap. None of this behavior is irrational; it is the rational response to a system that has never defined the lifespan of its own authorizations.

When cadence is governed, that pattern reverses, every commitment will be reviewed against current reality at predictable intervals. Leaders authorize work with clarity because the renewal rhythm protects the system from outdated obligations. The organization builds skill at decisive renewal rather than perpetual defense of sunk costs. Progress becomes visible and predictable because the work that remains active is the work that continues to warrant the effort sustaining it. This instrument does not constrain ambition. It channels it into execution the system can sustain. The organization that respects its temporal ceilings moves faster because it avoids the recovery cycles that consume more time than the original work itself. It compounds capability because completed and renewed commitments create the foundation for the next wave of growth. It preserves leadership bandwidth for directional judgment rather than revalidation.

When this renewal rhythm takes hold, the planning table changes character within one or two cycles: teams arrive with current assumptions rather than with defenses of expired ones, and the agenda shifts from justifying the past to governing the future.

The difference is structural. One organization operates as a collection of commitments that must be constantly re-justified at the center. The other operates as an integrated system whose authorizations carry explicit expiration and renewal points. The first depends on the continuous availability of people who can revalidate under pressure. The second depends on the design that makes revalidation structural and predictable.

Cadence as the lifespan of authorization is therefore not a limitation on vision. It is the condition that makes sustained strategic execution possible. When the system knows how long its commitments remain valid, it carries them reliably. When leadership governs renewal rather than arbitrating drift, attention returns to whether the system itself still warrants the effort sustaining it.

Every operation where I have put cadence in place showed the same result within two cycles. Strategic completion rates rose and resource allocation decisions held across quarters. Leadership meetings shortened because the agenda no longer included defense of expired assumptions. The system became self-regulating in the dimension of time, freeing leadership to focus on the dimensions that remain irreducibly human.

Sequence, load, and cadence together establish the complete foundation for orchestrated execution. They ensure that work enters in the right order, in the right volume, and for the right duration. The transition from carrying motion to governing the conditions that produce it begins here. Absence becomes evidence that the transition from operator to architect is underway.

PART FIVE
RELIABILITY WITHOUT PRESENCE

CHAPTER 14
WHEN ABSENCE BECOMES EVIDENCE

THE CONVERGENCE

The three governing instruments now operate as an integrated set. Sequence determines the order in which work enters motion. Load determines the volume the system can carry concurrently. Cadence determines how long any commitment remains valid once it is already moving. The three instruments together have converted execution from recovery into governed flow. The first evidence of that conversion appears in a specific moment. Now, the leader no longer supplies motion through personal presence but governs the conditions under which that motion sustains itself.

The first evidence of this shift appears in a specific moment. The leader steps away. The system continues.

Organizations reached this threshold across commercial operations and fulfillment networks in multiple markets. The crossing always looks the same from the inside. A P&L owner who had spent two years installing the governing instruments stepped away from daily operations for the first time in five years. He had planned the absence carefully, delegating authority across the three instruments and confirming that release gates, absorption ceilings, and renewal points were all active. The business was in the middle of a major capacity expansion, three new product lines were entering their first full quarter, and two key channel partners were renegotiating terms. From the outside the conditions looked volatile. Internally the system held because the instruments were in place.

He returned after four weeks to find that the expansion had progressed on schedule. The product lines had met their launch targets. The channel negotiations had closed within the original parameters. No escalation traffic had reached him during the absence. No emergency calls had interrupted the trip. The operational cadence had continued without interruption because the structure held the work in place. Strategic initiatives that had once required his direct involvement advanced through the governed logic now embedded in the system, and the architecture organized the arrangement while the orchestration instruments carried the motion.

The week you returned from travel to discover that the same decisions you would have made were made correctly in your absence. The planning cycle that closed on target without the usual last-minute interventions. The quarterly review where the integrated result improved rather than declined during your reduced visibility. The specific disorientation that follows is instructive. What arrives first is not relief but the quiet realization that the organization no longer requires your constant presence to remain coherent.

That realization marks the boundary between operator and architect.

When the instruments are absent, organizations compensate through leadership availability. Meetings multiply and decisions escalate as teams wait for the person who can restore coherence. The organization reads this activity as strong leadership, though the two operate differently. Leadership at scale prevents the problem from arising. Heroic intervention addresses it after it has arrived, and an organization dependent on heroic intervention builds skill at the wrong activity.

Absence becomes evidence because it reveals what the system can carry independently. When absence no longer creates degradation, the governing conditions have been transferred from personal presence to structural design. The system no longer waits for the leader to move it. It moves because the conditions required for motion have been designed into its logic.

I watched this shift take hold in a business I led across several markets. Before the instruments were installed, my calendar was the primary coordinating mechanism. Every strategic initiative, every cross-functional commitment, every adjustment to capacity or priority required my direct involvement to maintain alignment. After the instruments were installed, the calendar emptied of the work the system now carried. The disorientation lasted less than one cycle. What replaced it was the freedom to operate at the altitude the organization's ambition required.

The leadership role changes in a specific and immediate way. The leader no longer enters the work to restore coherence. The leader governs the design that makes coherence structural rather than personal. When this transition completes, the weekly meetings change character. What once functioned as triage begins focusing on whether the direction the system is advancing still warrants the effort sustaining it, whether the language encoding expectations retains the precision the architecture requires, and whether the renewal rhythms remain matched to the pace at which the environment is changing. These responsibilities cannot be designed into the system because they govern the validity of the system itself. What they are, precisely, is the subject of Chapter 16.

The difference becomes structural and visible. One organization continues to function only as long as the individuals stabilizing it remain present. The other continues to function because execution has been transferred into the design of the system itself. The first depends on tenure and consumes what it depends on. The second has moved past it, compounding rather than consuming. Durability is the final measure. The organization that depends on its leader to act can scale only as far as that leader's presence can extend. The organization whose leader holds the governing conditions under which execution remains legitimate can continue advancing beyond the tenure of any individual responsible for it. The design outlasts the designer.

This convergence manifests in concrete operational outcomes that leaders can measure directly. Delivery reliability stabilizes because load never exceeds absorptive capacity. Strategic initiatives complete on schedule because sequence prevents causal interference. Resource allocation decisions hold because cadence retires or renews authorization before assumptions expire. The organization no longer cycles between surge and recovery. Effort compounds because each completed commitment strengthens the foundation for the next. Strategic options widen because leadership attention is spent shaping future conditions rather than preserving current motion.

When this convergence takes hold, the same hidden costs disappear within one or two planning cycles. Before the instruments, every absence created a tax in delayed decisions, inflated contingency buffers, and escalated low-level issues that had no structural path to resolution. The before picture is familiar by now. After convergence, those costs vanish. The gains compound in ways the earlier chapters have already described, calendar time, confidence, escalation volume. Escalation volume drops because the system resolves routine work locally. The organization gains not only calendar time but the cognitive bandwidth that coordination overhead was consuming, and I have found that the recovery of that bandwidth is the change leaders feel most immediately and describe most consistently as the point when the transition became real for them.

This convergence also changes how the organization learns. When execution depends on personal intervention, feedback is filtered through the leader's presence and priorities, which means problems surface at the point they reach the center rather than at the point they originate. When execution runs on governed instruments, feedback arrives undistorted and at the point where the problem began. Root causes become visible rather than masked by the recovery that concealed them. The system compounds knowledge rather than resetting each quarter when a leader steps back in to restore coherence.

In a mid-sized fulfillment network operating across three countries, the P&L owner stepped away for a month during peak season. Prior to the instruments, the same absence would have triggered daily escalation calls and emergency reallocations. With the instruments in place, the network absorbed a twelve-percent volume spike without a single escalation. Buffer utilization stayed within the governed ceiling, renewal gates retired two low-value promotions automatically, and sequence logic released new promotions only after capacity cleared. The operation did not simply survive the absence; it improved its on-time delivery by three points. The leader returned to find the system had self-corrected in ways he had previously spent weeks forcing.

Ask yourself three questions after any period of reduced visibility: Did operational cadence continue without degradation? Did strategic initiatives advance without requiring re-authorization from the center? Did resource allocation decisions hold without arbitration? If the answer to all three is yes, absence has become evidence that the instruments are functioning. If any answer is no, the gap points directly to the instrument that still requires strengthening.

CHAPTER 15
FREEDOM THROUGH CONSTRAINT

THE RELEASE

A head of strategy at a multi-region industrial manufacturer spent eighteen months installing the governing instruments across a three-year plan. He had done the work correctly. The direction was set at the annual offsite. Operational planning refreshed quarterly. Execution priorities updated monthly. Early in each cycle, execution tracked strategic intent closely because authorization was recent and shared understanding intact. As the year progressed, operational decisions began optimizing against evolving market constraints while the strategic commitments themselves remained unchanged. The teams were responding rationally to the reality in front of them. The system was carrying the work without requiring constant realignment from above.

The leader expected to feel liberated. What he felt instead was temporary disorientation.

The inbox was quieter than it had been in years. Escalation traffic had dropped. The weekly rhythm continued without him restoring it. What remained was the work that lived outside the system's own logic: the judgment about whether the assumptions supporting the design remained legitimate. He told me he did not know what to do with the silence.

That disorientation is what this chapter is about.

When the governing instruments are in place, the motion of execution transfers into the design of the system. Commitments advance through governed sequence. Concurrency stays within the absorptive ceiling. Authorization renews before drift can accumulate. Leaders arrive at this point after years of architectural work and are still surprised by what happens next: the continuous intervention that once maintained coherence becomes unnecessary, because coherence now lives in the structure rather than in the availability of the person who built it. What the leader expected to feel as liberation arrives, at first, as unfamiliarity. The calendar has emptied of the work the system now carries. What remains is harder, quieter, and more consequential than anything that just left.

You have been through a version of this. The quarter when every function reported on track and the integrated result held without your direct involvement. The planning session where the team proposed trade-offs that aligned with both current conditions and long-term direction, and you had nothing to correct. The specific strangeness that follows is worth naming precisely: The responsibility operating at the right altitude, for the first time without competition from the work beneath it. Leadership attention that had been consumed by coordination goes back to directing rather than arbitrating.

When the instruments are absent, organizations run on personal constraint. Leaders insert themselves to maintain coherence, teams learn to wait for that insertion, and the organization interprets the pattern as strong oversight. Constraint through design prevents the problem from arising. Constraint through presence addresses it afterward. An organization built around the second never develops the capacity to carry its own motion, because the motion is always being supplied from the outside.

Freedom through constraint is what happens when that supply ends. The governing instruments create boundaries that release capability rather than restrict it. Teams operate with greater autonomy because the boundaries within which that autonomy holds are now structural and explicit. Decisions resolve at the point of work because accountability travels with the commitment rather than returning to the center. Progress compounds because each completed commitment builds absorptive capacity for what follows. The organization stops cycling between effort and recovery and begins to produce continuous throughput.

The shift took hold in the same industrial manufacturer once the instruments reached full operational density. Before they existed, strategic planning cycles were dominated by realignment conversations, the same priorities revisited three or four times because nothing structural had ever governed the order, volume, or lifespan of authorization. After they existed, those conversations stopped. The work the realignment had been doing moved into the system's logic. The leadership time that had been consumed by perpetual intervention became available for directional judgment and system design. The difference was measurable within a single cycle.

The character of every meeting the organization holds changes under this condition. Execution continues without continuous intervention, so the meetings no longer function as triage. They focus instead on whether the direction the system is advancing still warrants the effort sustaining it, whether the language encoding expectations retains the precision architecture requires, and whether the governing rhythms remain matched to the pace at which the environment is changing. These are harder questions than the ones they replaced, and they belong to a form of leadership that the coordination work used to crowd out entirely.

Four responsibilities remain. They are irreducible. That is the subject of the next chapter.

The organizations that reach this condition share a common characteristic. They no longer celebrate heroic intervention because heroic intervention has become unnecessary. They celebrate the quiet evidence of a system that carries its own work. Teams experience the freedom that comes from knowing the boundaries within which they can act with full authority. Leaders experience the freedom that comes from knowing their attention is required only where human judgment cannot be replaced by design.

Freedom through constraint is the release of organizational capability that occurs when the conditions of execution have been made structural rather than personal. Execution continues because the architecture carries it. The leader no longer carries execution. The leader governs what allows execution to sustain itself.

This is an elevation of accountability to the level the organization's ambition requires. The work that once consumed leadership time in coordination now proceeds independently. The work that remains is the work only leadership can perform: directional judgment, expectation fidelity, renewal calibration, and protection from structural debt.

The same shift appears each time this release takes hold. Operational cadence stabilized. Strategic initiatives completed without drift. Resource allocation decisions held across quarters. The organization no longer cycled between surge and recovery. Effort compounded because each completed commitment strengthened the foundation for the next. Optionality widened because leadership attention was spent shaping future conditions rather than preserving current motion.

The pattern showed most concretely in a commercial operation I led across Southeast Asia. The instruments had been installed for fourteen months when the regional director took a planned four-week absence during a critical pricing negotiation cycle. Before the instruments existed, the same absence would have produced daily status calls, re-approvals of every major commitment, and last-minute reallocations of shared marketing and supply-chain resources. With the instruments in place, the negotiation closed on the original timeline. Two low-value channel promotions were retired automatically at the renewal gate. The sequence logic released the next wave only after capacity cleared. The operation did not simply survive the absence; it improved gross margin by two points while reducing coordination overhead by thirty percent. The director returned to find that the system had executed decisions he would have made himself, without any of the usual escalation traffic reaching him.

That outcome is not exceptional leadership. It is what a governed system produces when it has been built correctly.

The hidden costs that disappear under this condition are substantial. Before the instruments, every absence created a tax: delayed decisions, inflated contingency buffers, escalated low-level issues that should have resolved locally. After the instruments are in place, those taxes vanish. Escalation volume drops because the system resolves routine work at the point it occurs. The organization gains calendar time, and more importantly, the cognitive bandwidth that perpetual triage consumes. Leaders stop managing interference and begin shaping the conditions that determine competitive advantage.

This release also changes how the organization learns. When execution depends on personal intervention, feedback is filtered through the leader's presence and priorities. When execution runs on governed instruments, feedback arrives undistorted, at the point of occurrence, before anyone in the center has a chance to absorb the noise. Problems surface faster. Root causes become visible rather than masked by heroic recovery. The system compounds knowledge rather than resetting each quarter when the next intervention cycle begins.

In practice, three changes become measurable within two planning cycles. Cycle time for strategic initiatives shortens because work no longer waits for the leader's availability. Resource productivity rises because capacity is protected rather than arbitrated. Leadership span of control expands because the system carries more work independently. Organizations that reach this point consistently report that the same leadership team can govern twice the complexity with substantially less coordination overhead. The gains are structural, and they hold across cycles rather than requiring the next intervention to sustain them.

The final test of this release is durability across leadership change. When a key executive departs, the system continues because the instruments remain. The incoming leader inherits a governed flow rather than a set of personal relationships that must be rebuilt from the beginning. This is the ultimate measure of structural work: it survives the builder. The organization no longer ties its capacity to any single individual's calendar or energy. It advances because the conditions for advancement have been designed into its logic and protected at the governing edge.

Freedom through constraint is the highest form of organizational maturity the preceding chapters have been building toward; now execution advances without the leader present to push it. The leader now defines the organization's reach by the quality of the governing design. What that form of leadership requires, and what it leaves irreducible, is the subject of Chapter 16.

CHAPTER 16
THE IRREDUCIBLE RESPONSIBILITIES

THE AUTHORITY

The system carries execution independently, the instruments are in place, three words carry the same transition without the repetition. Four responsibilities remain that no instrument can govern, because they govern the validity of the system itself.

In the operations I described in Chapter 14, those four responsibilities concentrated at a specific boundary. Across every organization where this transition completes, the same four responsibilities remained. They are the only work the design cannot absorb. Once the instruments are installed, the work that remains is not operational. It is the judgment about whether the assumptions supporting the design remain legitimate, and that judgment belongs to no structure.

You have reached this moment when the operational engine runs smoothly and the strategic questions become the only ones that require your judgment. The calendar has emptied of coordination work and filled with decisions only leadership can make. The authority that follows is custodianship, and it is harder to hold than the authority of presence was, because it offers no urgency signal to confirm that it is being exercised.

When the instruments are absent, organizations run on personal authority. Leaders insert themselves to maintain coherence, teams learn to wait for that insertion, and the organization reads the pattern as strong leadership. Authority through design prevents the problem from arising. Authority through presence addresses it afterward. An organization dependent on the second builds skill at the wrong activity, and builds it for years before the cost becomes visible.

The four irreducible responsibilities are these.

The first is directional evaluation: whether the direction the system is advancing still justifies the effort sustaining it. The system optimizes toward whatever destination it has been given. The leader determines independently whether that destination still warrants the journey. Markets shift while the system executes. Competitors move while the instruments hold sequence and load and cadence in place. The governing instruments cannot evaluate their own direction. Only the leader at the governing edge can weigh whether the current trajectory still warrants the resources being consumed, and that judgment requires external sensing no internal instrument can replicate.

The second is semantic integrity: preserving the density of language encoding expectations so that architecture continues functioning without interpretation. Precise language is the medium through which the system carries intent. As the density of governing language softens, expectations regain the elasticity that precise encoding was designed to eliminate. Vague commitments erode at every boundary they cross. Precise language survives transit. Governance migrates back into negotiation without any single event announcing that the regression has begun, and the leader must detect and correct that drift before it becomes visible in the numbers.

The third is temporal horizon calibration: maintaining the renewal rhythms governing commitments as the pace of external change evolves. What worked as a quarterly renewal rhythm in a stable market may need to become monthly in a volatile one. The governing instruments execute renewal at whatever frequency they have been calibrated to. The leader must determine whether that frequency remains appropriate as markets accelerate, technological cycles compress, or competitive volatility shortens the useful lifespan of strategic decisions.

The fourth is boundary protection: guarding the system from structural debt that would otherwise accumulate at the interfaces where work changes hands. Interfaces that once required constant negotiation must remain governed. Any drift here reintroduces the dependency the instruments were built to eliminate, incrementally, without announcement, in the small adjustments that each seem reasonable and together constitute a regression to the original condition.

These responsibilities cannot be delegated because they govern the validity of the system itself. They persist at the same intensity after the system is built as before, but they are now the only demands on leadership attention rather than a fraction of it buried beneath the coordination work the system has absorbed.

I have already described what that calendar looked like before the instruments were in place and what it looked like after. The disorientation of that transition lasted less than one cycle. What the four responsibilities described in this chapter require is different: they do not fill the calendar with coordination. They fill it with judgment that has no feedback loop until much later. Not ease. Altitude. The four responsibilities were harder to hold than anything the coordination work had demanded, because they required judgment that could not be confirmed until much later, often after conditions had already shifted.

The organizations that endure are the ones whose leaders built systems capable of continuing their work, not as a monument to the builder's effort but as evidence that the work was done correctly. When the leader steps away and execution continues without degradation, execution has been transferred from personal presence into the architecture itself. The system moves without being pushed, and protected at its governing edge by the four responsibilities that remain irreducibly human.

The difference between these two trajectories becomes structural and visible. The distinction between those two trajectories is what the four responsibilities are built to preserve.

Durability becomes the final measure. The organization whose leader holds the design accountable can continue advancing beyond the tenure of any individual responsible for it.

The system persists. The work persists.

The transition from operator to custodian marks the completion of the arc. Execution no longer depends on presence to remain coherent. Leadership remains accountable for the conditions that allow coherence to persist without it. The leader is present at a different level, holding the conditions under which the system remains legitimate rather than supplying the motion the system produces on its own. What survives across that transition is structure: held at its governing edge by judgment disciplined enough to preserve legitimacy once execution no longer requires supervision.

They are the work of custodianship. They keep the system legitimate rather than merely operational. They separate the architect from the operator long after the instruments have been installed.

The hidden costs that disappear under custodianship are substantial. Before the instruments, every leadership transition created a tax in lost momentum, rebuilt relationships, and relearned processes. Teams learned to wait for the new leader to reestablish alignment. Leaders learned to reinsert themselves to restore coherence. After custodianship is established, those taxes vanish. Teams continue to execute with confidence because the boundaries are structural. The incoming leader inherits a governed flow rather than a set of personal dependencies to rebuild. Escalation volume stays low because the system resolves routine work locally. The organization gains continuity, and beyond continuity, the ability to scale past any single individual's tenure.

Custodianship also changes how the organization evolves. When execution depends on personal authority, leadership change resets the system. When execution runs on governed instruments with custodianship at the edge, leadership change becomes an opportunity for refinement rather than a disruption. The incoming leader can focus immediately on the four irreducible responsibilities rather than rebuilding the foundation from the conditions the previous leader left. Knowledge compounds rather than resets. The system develops resilience to leadership transitions rather than fragility to them.

In practice, three changes become measurable once custodianship is established. Leadership transition risk drops because execution no longer depends on who occupies the governing role. Strategic agility increases because the leader's attention is spent on directional judgment rather than operational carrying. Organizational durability extends beyond any individual's tenure because the work is no longer tied to presence. These gains hold across leadership changes rather than resetting when the next cycle begins.

The final test of custodianship is durability across multiple leadership changes. When two or more key executives depart in succession and the system continues without degradation, custodianship has been proven. The organization advances because the design does.

The four irreducible responsibilities are the highest form of leadership accountability this book describes. They are the work of ensuring that execution remains legitimate. The leader who carries them no longer supplies motion. The leader governs the logic that keeps motion legitimate across time, across markets, and across generations of leadership.

The system carries the work. The leader carries the conditions that make the work legitimate. The Art of Managing Business Expectations reaches its conclusion when the leader can step away and the system continues, when absence becomes evidence, when freedom emerges through constraint, and when the only responsibilities that remain are the four that no design can replace. Execution advances independently. Leadership remains accountable at the governing edge.

Whether execution depends on you or survives you is the question Chapter 17 answers from the other side.

CHAPTER 17
CUSTODIAN

THE STEWARDSHIP

Years before I had language for it, I was living inside the condition this book describes. The work moved because I made it move. The results arrived because I was present to ensure they would. The organization performed, and the performance confirmed that the arrangement was working. It was working. It was also fragile in a way that scale would eventually expose, and fragile in a way that the results themselves prevented me from seeing.

What I came to understand, through the kind of experience that arrives before the explanation does, is that building a system capable of carrying execution is different in kind from carrying execution yourself. Both require genuine effort, but only one compounds. Only one produces something that continues to function when you are no longer supplying the force that drives it.

That understanding is what the preceding chapters have been building toward. This is where it lands.

• • •

Performance survives while sustainability erodes beneath it. Every experienced operator recognizes the condition from the opening chapter: results continuing to arrive, their continuity dependent on individuals who stabilize commitments and restore alignment whenever the system loses coherence under motion. The organization functions because people intervene wherever the structure has not been designed to carry what execution requires. That is where the book began, and this is where it ends. The distance between those two points is the subject of everything that came between them.

What the preceding chapters have shown is that this condition is rarely recognized as structural absence. It is interpreted through the explanations most available to leadership: competence gaps, coordination breakdowns, communication failures, inconsistent accountability. Each explanation directs corrective effort toward the people experiencing the consequences rather than toward the system generating those consequences. The organization becomes progressively more skilled at recovering coherence without ever reducing the frequency with which coherence must be recovered. The capability being built is the wrong one, and the results keep confirming it is the right one.

The first shift the book introduced was perceptual. Treating the organization as a collection of functions whose performance combines naturally into coherent results is the first diagnostic error this book addressed. Once the interface lens becomes available, the recurring pattern of unexplained variance begins to make sense: the organization is a system across which expectations must travel without losing meaning, and when they lose it, execution fragments regardless of how capable the people inside it are. Outcomes diverge because expectations lose precision as they cross boundaries the organization has never been designed to govern. Naming the condition correctly changes what the organization looks at when it tries to understand why execution keeps requiring the same interventions.

Architecture addresses the first structural absence. Expectations encoded with enough precision to survive translation across interfaces where work changes hands. Authority moving with commitments rather than waiting for escalation to reconnect it. Interfaces that once depended on informal coordination becoming governed pathways through which intent travels intact. The organization stops relying on individuals standing at those boundaries and starts relying on the design governing how work moves through them.

Yet architecture alone cannot sustain coherence once work begins moving through the system under the conditions scale imposes. Commitments enter motion in overlapping sequences. Concurrent initiatives compete for the same integrating capacity. Decisions authorized under one set of conditions remain active after those conditions have changed. The system that is structurally sound at rest begins to accumulate interference once motion begins, and that interference produces exactly the pattern the opening chapter described: intervention restores alignment, results arrive, and the dependency producing both stays invisible.

Orchestration addresses this second absence. Sequence determines the order in which commitments are permitted to enter motion, so that each new initiative finds stable ground rather than generating interference. Load governs the volume of concurrent commitments so that absorption capacity remains available for completion rather than being consumed by coordination overhead. Cadence governs the lifespan of authorization so that commitments remain valid as conditions evolve rather than persisting beyond the premises that justified them. Sequence prevents causal interference. Load prevents capacity interference. Cadence prevents temporal interference. When these instruments operate together, the system begins to carry execution without requiring the leader to supply the motion.

Organizations cross from the first condition into the second, and the crossing rarely announces itself. Escalation queues shorten. Calls that once required executives to reconnect the sequence become shorter and less frequent. Initiatives that used to wait for personal authorization begin advancing on their own schedule. What looks, from inside the old pattern, like a loss of connection is the system doing what it was designed to do. The leader can step away or redirect attention to strategic work without the execution stopping.

At this point the dependency the book has been diagnosing dissolves. Execution continues even when leadership presence recedes. What remains for leadership is legitimacy: the conditions under which the system continues to be worth running.

Architecture, orchestration, and cadence govern activity inside the system. The boundary between the system's internal logic and the conditions that determine whether that logic remains legitimate lies beyond what any instrument can reach. The system cannot determine whether it remains aligned with the conditions surrounding it, cannot evaluate whether the direction it advances still warrants the effort sustaining it, and cannot detect when the assumptions that made its governing design valid have shifted far enough that the design itself requires recalibration.

In the organizations I helped move past this threshold, what remained was not less work. It was work of a different kind entirely. The judgments that concentrated at the governing boundary were harder than the ones the system had absorbed, because they could not be verified through performance data. They required looking outward rather than inward, reading conditions the system itself had no instruments to measure.

Four responsibilities remain at that boundary. Strategic posture governs the exposure within which the organization operates. Directional integrity governs whether the path the system advances still warrants the effort sustaining it. Semantic integrity preserves the density of the language carrying expectations across boundaries, maintaining the precision that architecture depends on to function without interpretation. Temporal horizon calibration ensures that renewal rhythms remain matched to the pace at which reality changes, not the pace at which it was changing when the system was designed. These conditions govern the validity of the system itself and cannot be delegated to it.

No instrument governs that boundary. Leadership holds it.

Leadership changes character once the system is in place, and the change is worth being precise about. In the operator-centric organization, influence appears through visible activity. Leaders stabilize execution through intervention, and their value is confirmed by the problems that require their presence to resolve. In the governed organization, influence appears through the integrity the system maintains without intervention. The leader's contribution becomes visible through what the organization continues to hold intact when presence is not required.

No urgency signal arrives and no rescue moment follows. There is continuity instead, produced by conditions the leader holds at the governing boundary, invisible in the moment and cumulative over time.

The leaders who adapted most quickly, in every case the leaders who adapted most quickly were the ones who had already stopped confusing urgency with importance. The ones who struggled longest were the ones whose professional identity had been built entirely around the visible confirmation that judgment had just mattered. That confirmation disappears in a governed system. What replaces it is harder to see and more important to sustain.

I have seen both trajectories play out across the same industry, sometimes in organizations competing for the same customers. One sustains outcomes through escalation and recovery, consuming capability to maintain continuity, resetting with each intervention because the system never completes a full cycle without disruption. The other builds capability with each cycle because execution no longer depends on being rescued. Over several cycles the trajectories diverge in a way that becomes unmistakable, because one is consuming what it depends on while the other is compounding it.

Management's purpose therefore changes once this condition becomes visible. Management is the design and maintenance of the conditions under which expectations retain meaning, commitments remain coherent, and execution advances without requiring continuous stabilization. Organizations that optimize for coordination and supervision without addressing the structural conditions governing how expectations travel will keep finding themselves in the same place: capable people working hard, results arriving, and dependency deepening beneath the performance that conceals it. What the organization can do depends on the design rather than on who happens to be present.

The system carries execution. Leadership carries legitimacy.

Operator and custodian are worth naming precisely, because the words matter at this distance. The operator carries execution. The custodian holds what allows execution to carry itself. What changes between those two roles is what responsibility means at the level of leadership that organizations actually need: someone who builds a system that holds together in their absence, rather than someone whose presence is the reason it holds.

The operators I have worked with across five countries and more than two decades recognized this transition at different speeds, but the ones who made it described the same experience. The work became less visible and more consequential. The interventions that once confirmed importance were gone. What remained was the quality of judgment they brought to boundaries the system could not observe, and that judgment determined whether the organization's accumulated capability continued to compound or began to erode.

The leader who has followed the full progression of this argument arrives at a form of accountability the operator-centered organization cannot see from inside its own operating rhythm. Execution is no longer what the leader must supply, because the system now carries that responsibility. What requires continuous judgment is whether the assumptions allowing the system to function remain aligned with the reality the organization inhabits. That question renews rather than resolves.

Strategic posture, directional integrity, semantic integrity, temporal horizon calibration: these four conditions govern the validity of the system itself. Each requires sustained attention. None can be delegated to the system they govern.

Execution reliability is a structural property. The legitimacy of that structure remains a leadership responsibility. Both are necessary, and each depends on the other.

The difference between these trajectories emerges across cycles: the organization that carries execution becomes increasingly dependent on the individuals stabilizing it, while the organization that governs execution becomes increasingly independent of them. Both may look equally strong at the beginning. The divergence widens with every cycle that passes.

Durability is what separates the two trajectories. Not performance in a given period, not the strength of the leadership team at a particular moment, but whether the organization continues to function when the conditions present during its best years are no longer available. Organizations whose coherence depends on particular individuals endure only as long as those individuals remain present to supply it. When they leave or redirect their attention, the coherence they were supplying leaves with them. The organization returns to the condition described in the opening chapter: dependency deepening beneath the performance that conceals it, people absorbing costs the system was never designed to acknowledge that were never built to sustain themselves.

Organizations built to carry execution through governing design continue functioning beyond the tenure of the leaders who created them. The system persists because the design persists. What was built does not require the builder to remain present for it to keep working.

Whether execution depends on you or survives you is the ultimate test of leadership.

FROM OPERATOR TO ARCHITECT

For a period of time strong operators sustain performance through presence, judgment, and intervention. They reconnect what drifts. They resolve what stalls. They stabilize what the system has not yet learned to hold. That phase produces results. It also produces the dependency that eventually limits them.

Most operators do not see the dependency forming. The results confirm the approach. The intervention works. The organization advances. The pattern reinforces itself until scale exposes what proximity was concealing.

At scale the question changes. It is whether execution continues when the operator is no longer present to carry it. That question marks the boundary between two forms of leadership that look similar from the outside and differ entirely in what they produce over time.

I have been on both sides of that boundary. The difference is not subtle once you have crossed it. On one side the organization moves because you move it. On the other the organization moves because it has been built to move. The results can look identical in any given quarter. What they are building toward is entirely different.

The transition has a precise shape. Expectations move from being interpreted at every boundary to being encoded before they enter the system. Decisions move from being escalated for resolution to being transmitted with the authority required to resolve them locally. Execution moves from being personally sustained to being structurally governed.

When those shifts hold something unfamiliar appears. The system begins to carry what the leader once carried. Leadership concentrates at the level where design cannot reach and delegation cannot extend. The involvement has moved to a different layer, the layer where the system's governing logic lives.

Organizations that depend on intervention consume leadership capacity with each cycle. Organizations that govern through structure compound it. The difference between those two trajectories does not appear in a single quarter. It appears in the widening distance between what one organization can sustain and what another has been built to produce. One organization is always paying the cost of its own coherence. The other is building on it.

For operators entering this transition the work becomes specific. Define expectations with enough precision that they survive the distance between decision and delivery. Govern the sequence in which work enters the system so that effort compounds rather than collides. Regulate the load the system carries so that capacity is not consumed faster than it can be restored. Establish cadence so that commitments renew before they expire and execution remains anchored to conditions that still hold. And hold the boundary that none of those instruments can govern themselves: whether the system remains pointed toward something worth building.

That last responsibility is the one most easily neglected once the system is running well. The instruments govern motion, volume, and renewal. They cannot evaluate the destination. That judgment belongs to the leader alone, and it requires the kind of sustained attention that operational carrying rarely leaves room for. One of the less-discussed benefits of the transition is that it creates the space for that judgment to be exercised without interruption.

Few organizations ever complete this transition, not because it is impossible and not because the leaders inside those organizations lack capability, but because the condition that makes the transition necessary is invisible for so long that the urgency to address it arrives late, after scale has already converted what was manageable into something structural.

The organizations that do complete it share something in common. Their leaders recognized, before the cost became obvious, that carrying execution and governing execution are different forms of work. They chose the latter not because it was easier but because they understood what it would make possible.

Structural leadership. The operator has become architect. The architecture, when built correctly, produces outcomes the operator no longer needs to personally carry. The system has been designed to carry them forward independently, across functions, across time, and across the departure of the individuals who built it.

That is the transition the preceding pages described. This is what it looks like from the other side.

GLOSSARY

THE EXPECTATION LEXICON

Glossary

The Expectation Lexicon

A Structural Language for Execution Integrity

Organizations rarely lack effort, intelligence, or commitment. What they often lack is language precise enough to describe the structural conditions governing whether execution remains coherent.

Each term in this lexicon names a structural reality that experienced leaders often sense but struggle to isolate with precision. The sensing arrives through operational experience; the naming makes the condition addressable. Once the language becomes available, the system becomes visible, and what is visible can be built.

The entries follow the same progression as the book: foundational constructs, structural perception, failure signatures, diagnostic instruments, governing instruments, and custodial accountability. A reader who has moved through the argument will find familiar territory here. A reader who begins here will find a map for the argument that follows.

FOUNDATIONAL CONSTRUCTS

The language underlying execution

Expectation A bounded unit of operational intent carrying scope, obligation, and consequence across time and organizational boundaries. *Operating line: Execution moves through expectations.*

Expectation Density The level of informational precision encoded when an expectation is created. High density means the expectation can travel without requiring reconstruction. Low density means it will require interpretation at every boundary it crosses. *Operating line: Low density invites interpretation.*

Expectation Fidelity The degree to which an expectation preserves its meaning as it travels across roles, functions, and time. Fidelity belongs to the medium carrying the expectation, not to the expectation at the moment it is expressed. The same words, moving through a poorly designed medium, arrive at a different destination than the one intended. *Operating line: Execution reliability equals expectation fidelity.*

Expectation Transmission The structural process through which expectations propagate across the organization. When transmission is designed, expectations arrive intact. When transmission is informal, expectations arrive as approximations. *Operating line: Execution succeeds when expectations survive the journey.*

Expectation Carriage The medium through which expectations travel. Personal carriage means expectations depend on individuals who interpret, reconnect, and stabilize meaning as the expectation moves. Architectural carriage means expectations move through structure that preserves meaning without requiring individual judgment at every transfer point. *Operating line: If people carry expectations, scale will eventually break them.*

Expectation Depreciation The loss of operational meaning as expectations cross organizational boundaries. Transmission loss is degradation through communication channels, where precision erodes as the signal travels. Translation loss is degradation when ownership transfers, where meaning shifts as context changes. *Operating line: Meaning erodes at boundaries.*

Expectation Saturation The condition in which concurrent commitments exceed the system's integrative capacity. The system stays active, but its ability to carry individual commitments to completion degrades because the integration capacity that completion requires is being consumed by the overhead of managing concurrency. *Operating line: Too many commitments create structural noise.*

Structural Fidelity The system's ability to preserve expectation integrity under scale and pressure. Structural fidelity is the aggregate property produced when architecture, orchestration, and cadence operate together to protect meaning in transit. *Operating line: Structure protects meaning.*

DIAGNOSTIC INSTRUMENTS

Portable tests for structural reliability

Dependency Signal Performance deteriorates when specific individuals become unavailable. The dependency signal is the clearest test of whether execution is structural or personal. If the system holds when people leave the room, the system exists. If it degrades, the people were the system. *Operating line: If performance disappears when a person leaves the room, the system was never there.*

False Cause Test An explanation is compensatory rather than structural when the improvement it produces cannot be sustained without repeating the effort that produced it. Capability initiatives that must be repeated, motivation programs that must be renewed, alignment sessions that must be conducted again: each signals that effort is performing work structure has never been designed to carry. *Operating line: Temporary fixes reveal the wrong diagnosis.*

Substitution Pattern Reliability exists only through the continuous involvement of specific individuals. The substitution pattern is present whenever removing those individuals from a process causes the process to degrade. The architecture that requires them is the problem. *Operating line: People are replacing the architecture.*

Carrying Threshold The point at which recovery improves while the need for recovery remains unchanged. When organizations become faster at fixing the same categories of problems without reducing the rate at which those problems occur, they have crossed the carrying threshold. Structural reliability means reducing the rate of occurrence, not accelerating recovery from it. *Operating line: Recovery speed cannot replace structural reliability.*

Expectation Fidelity Test Uneven outcomes across similar conditions indicate transmission failure rather than capability failure. When the same directive produces strong results in one area and costly variance in another with no consistent pattern, the variable is the medium carrying the expectation, not the people receiving it. *Operating line: Variance reveals the medium.*

Alignment Inspection Alignment that cannot be verified independently of the people reporting it. When leadership cannot inspect whether intent has been translated into consistent operational meaning without asking the people responsible for that translation, alignment remains a belief rather than a verified condition, and beliefs perform while verification would expose them. *Operating line: Alignment must be observable.*

FAILURE SIGNATURES

Parts I and II: When management stops scaling

Execution Drift Gradual divergence between encoded intent and operational reality. Drift originates in the loss of expectation precision in transit, accumulating across boundaries until the gap between what was decided and what is being executed becomes visible only when results expose it. *Operating line: Drift begins when expectations lose precision.*

Informal Debt The structural cost accumulated when teams compensate for missing architecture. Like financial debt, informal debt accrues interest. The compensation that prevents a structural problem from becoming visible today increases the cost of addressing it tomorrow. *Operating line: Improvisation accumulates interest.*

Shadow System An informal operating mechanism created to sustain throughput when formal structure fails. Shadow systems keep work moving by absorbing the variance that would otherwise expose where the structure requires redesign, which is precisely why they are so expensive. *Operating line: Shadow systems keep work moving while hiding the real problem.*

Structural Substitution The condition in which leadership presence performs functions that architecture should support. When structural substitution is the operating condition, execution depends on the availability of specific individuals rather than on the integrity of the system they sustain. *Operating line: Intervention replaces design.*

Competence Trap A reinforcing pattern in which capable individuals sustain results long enough to conceal structural weaknesses. The trap closes when the organization mistakes the quality of the people compensating for the system for the quality of the system itself. *Operating line: Strong people delay structural correction.*

Ghost Responsibility The condition in which operators are held accountable for outcomes derived from plans they had no hand in constructing. Accountability travels downward. Authorship does not follow. Operating line: Responsibility without authorship produces reactive execution.

Competence Inversion The moment when expertise becomes a constraint because execution waits for interpretation. When capable individuals become the bottleneck rather than the accelerant, competence has inverted: what once multiplied capacity now limits it. *Operating line: Judgment becomes the bottleneck.*

Heroism Tax The systemic cost of relying on decisive intervention instead of structural reliability. The heroism tax is paid twice: once for the intervention required to restore the outcome, and once for the structural improvement that the intervention displaced. *Operating line: Heroism is expensive.*

Rescue Cycle A reinforcing pattern in which leadership intervention becomes the default mechanism for securing outcomes. Once the rescue cycle is established, the organization calibrates its operating thresholds around the expectation of rescue, and the system learns to wait for it rather than resolve situations independently. *Operating line: Rescue teaches the system to wait.*

Alignment Theater The appearance of coordination in an environment where coordination cannot be structurally verified. Alignment theater emerges because the system has no mechanism for distinguishing confident expression from operational precision, so confident expression substitutes for it. The performers are sincere. The stage is empty. *Operating line: Alignment requires verification, not just agreement.*

P&L Hidden Tax The cumulative economic cost of the competence tax, heroism tax, and alignment tax operating simultaneously. The hidden tax distributes itself across the organization's operating capacity, in leadership bandwidth consumed, in learning deferred, and in strategic options narrowed by the cost of sustaining coherence through intervention. It accumulates steadily before appearing in the numbers. *Operating line: Structural failure eventually appears in the numbers.*

STRUCTURAL PERCEPTION

Part III: Seeing the organization differently

Management Architecture The structural arrangement governing how expectations are encoded, transmitted, verified, and renewed. Architecture determines whether execution depends on the judgment of individuals positioned at boundaries or on the design governing how work moves through them. *Operating line: Architecture determines whether execution depends on people or structure.*

Interface A boundary where expectation ownership transfers between roles, teams, or functions. Interfaces are where execution coherence is determined. They appear on no organizational chart, yet they govern what the chart produces. *Operating line: Execution reliability is decided at the handoff.*

Interface Topology The pattern of ownership transitions across the organization. The interface topology is the organization's actual operating system, distinct from the formal hierarchy. Understanding it is a prerequisite for governing it. *Operating line: The organization runs where work changes hands.*

Interface Lens A shift from viewing the organization as a set of functions to viewing it as a system of expectation transfers. The interface lens makes visible what the functional lens conceals: that outcomes are determined by what happens between functions, not by what happens inside them. *Operating line: Organizations are interfaces. Functions are only part of the picture.*

Informal Coordination Ad-hoc reconciliation of degraded expectations through conversation, escalation, or intervention. Informal coordination compensates for structural absence. It is rational, effective in the short term, and expensive at scale. *Operating line: Conversation compensates for missing structure.*

Structural Carrying The condition in which execution advances through architecture rather than intervention. When structural carrying is present, the system sustains coherence without requiring specific individuals to supply it. This is the condition the book is built to describe and produce. *Operating line: A system carries execution when people no longer have to.*

Signal Suppression Cost The learning deficit created when informal workarounds hide structural failures. Every time a capable individual bridges a gap the structure was never designed to carry, the signal that would have forced structural redesign is absorbed and lost. The organization receives the outcome without receiving the information that would explain how it was preserved. *Operating line: Workarounds silence the signals that force improvement.*

GOVERNING INSTRUMENTS

Part IV: From action to orchestration

Orchestration The discipline governing how work moves through the organization under real operating conditions. Architecture governs arrangement and orchestration governs motion, each necessary, neither substituting for the other. *Operating line: Execution reliability requires governing motion.*

Sequence The order in which commitments enter execution. When sequence is governed, effort compounds through causal readiness. When sequence is absent, initiatives that are individually sound begin interfering with one another the moment they occupy the same system simultaneously. *Operating line: Work must enter motion in the right order.*

Release Gate The structural decision point determining whether work begins. The release gate governs entry into motion based on two conditions: whether work is entering in the correct causal order, and whether the system has enough absorptive capacity to receive it without degrading what is already in motion. *Operating line: Some work must wait to start.*

Collision Tax The economic cost created when work enters motion without sequencing discipline. The collision tax is the cost of doing things in the wrong order, converting effort that should compound into interference that must be managed, at the expense of the initiatives already in motion. *Operating line: Unsequenced work collides.*

Absorption Capacity The system's ability to integrate concurrent commitments without destructive friction. Absorption capacity is defined by what the system can carry to completion without degrading the flow already in motion, a measure of integrative throughput, not of approved budgets, headcount, or available hours. *Operating line: Capacity governs concurrency.*

Absorption Ceiling The point beyond which additional work degrades throughput. The ceiling is observable: completion rates decline even as activity levels rise, escalation volume increases without a corresponding increase in novel decisions, and cycle times elongate across unrelated workstreams because integrating capacity is being consumed by interference rather than applied to resolution. *Operating line: More work can produce less progress.*

Cadence The rhythm through which commitments are reviewed, renewed, or concluded. Cadence governs the temporal validity of authorization, how long a commitment remains legitimate before it must be verified against current conditions. Without cadence, commitments accumulate rather than refresh, and execution organizes itself around directions that no longer hold. *Operating line: Commitments must expire.*

Renewal Boundary The moment at which active commitments are revalidated against current conditions. At the renewal boundary, a commitment must produce one of three outcomes: reaffirmation because its conditions remain valid, adjustment because conditions have evolved, or retirement because the premises authorizing it no longer exist. The renewal boundary is the structural verification point at which the system determines whether authorization remains legitimate, a governing mechanism, not a status meeting. *Operating line: Time resets authorization.*

Drift Tax The cost created when commitments persist longer than their assumptions. Resources remain committed to initiatives whose justification has expired. Decisions optimize against premises that are no longer current. Coordination effort rises as teams negotiate which commitments still apply, a conversation that becomes continuous when authorization carries no governed expiration. *Operating line: Expired decisions create friction.*

CUSTODIAL ACCOUNTABILITY

Part V: Reliability without presence

Governing Inversion The condition in which execution continues without leadership presence. The condition in which the system carries execution while leadership holds what the system cannot govern: the validity of the system itself. The system carries execution. Leadership holds the conditions under which the system remains legitimate. *Operating line: The system now carries execution.*

Strategic Posture Leadership's explicit judgment regarding acceptable exposure to uncertainty, volatility, and risk relative to the organization's ambition and capital structure. Strategic posture must be held as an explicit judgment because operational performance occurs inside the posture rather than defining it. When posture is held clearly, the organization can act with confidence. When posture is absent, the organization oscillates between expansion and retreat in ways no operational metric can diagnose. *Operating line: Exposure is a leadership decision.*

Directional Integrity Assessment of whether accumulated effort still converges toward a worthwhile objective. Directional integrity requires leadership to evaluate whether the destination the system is advancing toward still warrants the journey. The system can optimize for progress toward a destination. Leadership must determine independently whether the destination still merits the optimization. *Operating line: Effort must still point somewhere meaningful.*

Semantic Integrity Preservation of language precise enough to prevent interpretive drift. Over time, governing language loses density. Expectations drift back toward elasticity. Governance returns to negotiation without any single event announcing the regression. The regression announces itself in the numbers, not at the point it begins. Semantic integrity requires leadership to maintain the precision that architecture depends on before that regression becomes visible in the numbers. *Operating line: Precision protects execution.*

Temporal Horizon Calibration Alignment between internal decision rhythms and the pace of external change. Cadence can execute renewal at whatever frequency it has been calibrated to, but leadership must determine whether that frequency remains appropriate as markets accelerate, technological cycles compress, or competitive volatility shortens the useful lifespan of strategic decisions. Temporal horizon calibration is the judgment that keeps the cadence mechanism matched to the environment it is governing. *Operating line: Timing governs relevance.*

Custodianship The leadership responsibility that remains once execution carries itself. The custodian holds four things: the exposure boundary, the direction, the language, and the temporal rhythms that together determine whether the system remains legitimate. Custodianship is the form leadership takes when the system has been built correctly, concentrated at the boundary between the system's internal logic and the conditions that determine whether that logic remains valid. *Operating line: Custodians protect legitimacy, not activity.*

www.ingramcontent.com/pod-product-compliance
Lightning Source LLC
LaVergne TN
LVHW010951110826
845149LV00015B/3302

9798995732105